■SCHOLASTIC

Math Problem of the Day
Practice Mats

Mary Rosenberg

New York • Toronto • London • Auckland • Sydney
Mexico City • New Delhi • Hong Kong • Buenos Aires

Teaching *Resources*

Dedication

To Buttons.
You will live forever in our hearts.

Edited and produced by Immacula A. Rhodes
Cover design by Maria Lilja
Interior illustrations by Maxie Chambliss
Interior design by Holly Grundon and Sydney Wright

ISBN–13: 978-0-545-02813-4
ISBN–10: 0-545-02813-2

Contents

Introduction 5

How to Use the Practice Mats 5

Helpful Hints 7

Connections With the NCTM Standards 8

Addition

Math Problem of the Day 1 – 5
Writing Addition Sentences

Math Problem of the Day 6 – 10
Using Number Lines to Add

Math Problem of the Day 11 – 15
Solving Addition Word Problems

Subtraction

Math Problem of the Day 16 – 20
Writing Subtraction Sentences

Math Problem of the Day 21 – 25
Using Number Lines to Subtract

Math Problem of the Day 26 – 30
Solving Subtraction Word Problems

Numbers and Numeration

Math Problem of the Day 31 – 34
Comparing Numbers

Math Problem of the Day 35
Identifying Even Numbers

Math Problem of the Day 36
Identifying Odd Numbers

Math Problem of the Day 37
Identifying Odd and Even Numbers

Math Problem of the Day 38 – 43
Using Deductive Reasoning

Math Problem of the Day 44 – 47
Identifying Sets

Math Problem of the Day 48 – 50
Creating Sets

Math Problem of the Day 51 – 55
Identifying Place Value

Patterns and Shapes

Math Problem of the Day 56 – 67
Identifying Patterns

Math Problem of the Day 68 – 71
Drawing Shapes

Math Problem of the Day 72 – 73
Identifying Shapes

Math Problem of the Day 74
Recognizing Shapes

Math Problem of the Day 75 – 78
Making Shapes

Math Problem of the Day 79
Identifying Shapes and Sizes

Math Problem of the Day 80
Identifying Symmetry in Shapes

Math Problem of the Day 81 – 86
Drawing and Comparing Shapes

Math Problem of the Day 87 – 89
Transforming Shapes

Math Problem of the Day 90
Composing and Decomposing Shapes

Contents

Map Skills and Location

Math Problem of the Day 91 – 95
Identifying Compass Directions

Math Problem of the Day 96 – 100
Using Coordinates

Word Problems

Math Problem of the Day 101 – 115
Solving Word Problems

Measurement

Math Problem of the Day 116 – 119
Measuring Length

Math Problem of the Day 120
Measuring Height

Math Problem of the Day 121 – 125
Using a Calendar

Money

Math Problem of the Day 126 – 129
Adding Coins

Math Problem of the Day 130
Adding Money

Charts, Graphs, and Diagrams

Math Problem of the Day 131 – 133
Analyzing Charts

Math Problem of the Day 134 – 142
Using Graphs

Math Problem of the Day 143 – 152
Creating Graphs

Math Problem of the Day 153 – 156
Applying Concepts of Probability

Math Problem of the Day 157 – 161
Using Venn Diagrams

Fractions

Math Problem of the Day 162 – 163
Dividing Wholes Into Fractions

Problem Solving

Math Problem of the Day 164 – 168
Using Deductive Reasoning

Math Problem of the Day 169 – 173
Comparing Attributes

Math Problem of the Day 174 – 180
Using Graphic Organizers

Answer Key 191

Introduction

Welcome to *Math Problem of the Day Practice Mats*! The 180 fun, interactive math mats in this book are designed to engage your kindergarten and first grade students in the learning process, develop a love of and for math, and build essential math skills every day of the school year.

Each reproducible practice mat can be used to supplement and enhance your math curriculum as well as provide a starting point for teaching key mathematical concepts. The activities help students learn the important math skills addressed by the National Council of Teachers of Mathematics (NCTM) standards and curriculum focal points for kindergarten and first grade. Math topics within those content and process standards include addition, subtraction, patterns, geometry, money, measurement, place value, time, and graphing. Within each topic, the practice mats address similar skills and concepts using a variety of approaches, providing students with opportunities to learn according to their individual learning styles. In addition, your students will love the math activities!

How to Use the Practice Mats

The pages in *Math Problem of the Day Practice Mats* are designed to be used in a variety of settings and situations. Simply photocopy the practice mats you want to cover with students and you're ready to go! The only other materials needed for the activities are pencils and crayons.

Each practice mat is divided into two parts. A math problem or concept is featured on the main area of the mat. Students may need to solve problems, draw pictures, or use the information in this section to answer questions. An extra follow-up or "Quick Review" activity, which provides students with basic or previously taught skills, is on the left side of the page.

Here are some ways you might use *Math Problem of the Day Practice Mats* in your classroom:

- **Preview and review:** Practice mats provide a great way to introduce new concepts or skills, track students' progress in mastering essential math skills, and review concepts already covered in class.

- **Learning center activities:** You can select, photocopy, and assemble the desired practice mats into individual learning packets. For example, all of the pages under the topic of "Measurement" can be assembled to supplement a unit on measurement when students are doing individual activities in a learning center.

- **Paired or group activities:** Many of the practice mats work well as group assignments. For example, those that require the development of graphs allow students to work together to gather data and learn from each other. The deductive reasoning problems are also natural activities for pairs or groups since the questions prompt discussion of possibilities.

- **Quick checks:** The practice mats can be used as ready-to-use diagnostic tools. The problems provide a quick and easy way to see if students already know a concept before you begin teaching it or if they are grasping the concept while you are teaching your unit. Students aren't likely to feel that they are being "tested" because the activities are engaging and enjoyable.

- **Homework:** Parents and students will find that the practice mats are easy to use and enhance learning. The skill highlighted at the top of each mat helps parents see the math topics their children are studying. In addition, the activity gives children an opportunity to show their parents what they are learning, what they've mastered, and where they might need some extra guidance.

Helpful Hints

The following are some suggestions to make using the practice mats enjoyable for both you and your students:

- The first few times students use the practice mats, show them how the page is set up and guide them through completing the activities. Have them do the activity on the main area of the mat first and then complete the "Quick Review" activity.

- Invite students to develop stories that show how numbers can be used in real-life or imaginative settings. For example, have students tell a story about the two sets of dogs on the first practice mat. They might describe a simple story in which three dogs meet two more dogs sitting by a tree in the park. After becoming friends the five dogs begin to play chase around the park benches. The more students use words to help them understand numbers, the more fluent they will be in both expressive language and mathematics.

- Review what a compass rose is and how it is used before students begin work on the practice mats that focus on compass directions. Check that they understand the position of each direction and can identify objects that are located in each direction when they use their own location as a point of reference.

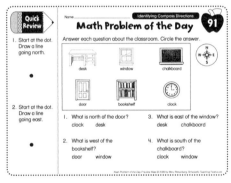

- When you introduce students to the mats that provide practice in using coordinates, show them how to trace the horizontal and vertical lines with their finger to find the point of intersection for specific coordinates. Ask them to identify which item is at that location and then write the name beside the coordinates at the right.

- The first time students encounter practice mats with graphic organizers, show them how to place Xs in boxes as they narrow choices. For example, on practice mat 178, help students see that once they learn that Sasha does not wear tall hats or helmets, they should draw Xs in the columns for these two hats for Sasha.

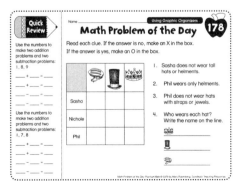

- Encourage your students to color the practice mats after they've completed the activities on the pages. Provide students with colored pencils, markers, and crayons.

- Once students are comfortable with the format of the practice mats, have them develop their own. Make copies for their classmates and have a "Homemade Math Problem of the Day" event to celebrate their accomplishments in mathematics over the course of the year.

Connections With the NCTM Standards

The activity pages in *Math Problem of the Day Practice Mats* are linked with the NCTM's content and process standards on the kindergarten and first grade levels. As the NCTM suggests, the practice mats teach these skills in a real-world context. Important math skills and concepts are not taught as abstractions, but as situations that children encounter and problem solve in their daily lives.

For easy reference as you plan your daily lessons, you'll find the primary skill on which the main activity focuses at the top of each practice mat. As you'll note, most pages include several activities and address more than one of the NCTM standards, providing your students with opportunities to practice other skills as well as the skill you are currently teaching. In addition, your students will build on what they have learned previously by using, for example, their experience in comparing numbers in the early practice mats to understand the reasoning required to find mystery numbers in later practice mats.

The activity pages in this book cover many of the NCTM standards for content and processes: number and operation; patterns, functions, and algebra; geometry and spatial sense; measurement; data analysis, statistics and probability; problem solving; reasoning and proof; communication; connections; and representation. Check the skills matrix on pages 9–10 to find the skills on which each practice mat focuses.

Enjoy using *Math Problem of the Day Practice Mats* and seeing how much your students look forward to learning mathematics in this fun and interactive format!

Connections With the NCTM Standards

Left Table (Addition, Subtraction, Numbers and Numeration)

	Content Standards					Process Standards				
	Number and Operation	Patterns, Functions, and Algebra	Geometry and Spatial Sense	Measurement	Data Analysis, Statistics, and Probability	Problem Solving	Reasoning and Proof	Communication	Connections	Representation
Addition										
Math Problem of the Day 1	◆							◆		◆
Math Problem of the Day 2	◆							◆		◆
Math Problem of the Day 3	◆							◆		◆
Math Problem of the Day 4	◆							◆		◆
Math Problem of the Day 5	◆							◆		◆
Math Problem of the Day 6	◆		◆					◆	◆	◆
Math Problem of the Day 7	◆		◆					◆	◆	◆
Math Problem of the Day 8	◆		◆					◆	◆	◆
Math Problem of the Day 9	◆		◆					◆	◆	◆
Math Problem of the Day 10	◆		◆					◆	◆	◆
Math Problem of the Day 11	◆							◆	◆	◆
Math Problem of the Day 12	◆							◆	◆	◆
Math Problem of the Day 13	◆							◆	◆	◆
Math Problem of the Day 14	◆							◆	◆	◆
Math Problem of the Day 15	◆						◆	◆	◆	◆
Subtraction										
Math Problem of the Day 16	◆							◆		◆
Math Problem of the Day 17	◆							◆		◆
Math Problem of the Day 18	◆							◆		◆
Math Problem of the Day 19	◆							◆		◆
Math Problem of the Day 20	◆							◆		◆
Math Problem of the Day 21	◆	◆				◆		◆	◆	◆
Math Problem of the Day 22	◆	◆				◆		◆	◆	◆
Math Problem of the Day 23	◆	◆				◆		◆	◆	◆
Math Problem of the Day 24	◆	◆				◆		◆	◆	◆
Math Problem of the Day 25	◆	◆				◆		◆	◆	◆
Math Problem of the Day 26	◆					◆		◆		◆
Math Problem of the Day 27	◆					◆		◆		◆
Math Problem of the Day 28	◆					◆		◆		◆
Math Problem of the Day 29	◆					◆		◆		◆
Math Problem of the Day 30	◆					◆		◆		◆
Numbers and Numeration										
Math Problem of the Day 31	◆						◆	◆		◆
Math Problem of the Day 32	◆						◆	◆		◆
Math Problem of the Day 33	◆						◆	◆		◆
Math Problem of the Day 34	◆						◆	◆		◆
Math Problem of the Day 35	◆	◆				◆		◆		◆
Math Problem of the Day 36	◆	◆				◆		◆		◆
Math Problem of the Day 37	◆							◆		◆
Math Problem of the Day 38	◆					◆	◆			
Math Problem of the Day 39	◆					◆	◆			
Math Problem of the Day 40	◆					◆	◆	◆		◆
Math Problem of the Day 41	◆					◆	◆	◆		◆
Math Problem of the Day 42	◆					◆	◆	◆		◆
Math Problem of the Day 43	◆					◆	◆	◆		◆
Math Problem of the Day 44	◆							◆		◆
Math Problem of the Day 45	◆							◆		◆
Math Problem of the Day 46	◆							◆		◆

Right Table (Patterns and Shapes, Map Skills and Location)

	Content Standards					Process Standards				
	Number and Operation	Patterns, Functions, and Algebra	Geometry and Spatial Sense	Measurement	Data Analysis, Statistics, and Probability	Problem Solving	Reasoning and Proof	Communication	Connections	Representation
Math Problem of the Day 47	◆							◆		◆
Math Problem of the Day 48	◆							◆		◆
Math Problem of the Day 49	◆							◆		◆
Math Problem of the Day 50	◆							◆		◆
Math Problem of the Day 51	◆					◆		◆	◆	◆
Math Problem of the Day 52	◆					◆		◆	◆	◆
Math Problem of the Day 53	◆							◆	◆	◆
Math Problem of the Day 54	◆							◆	◆	◆
Math Problem of the Day 55	◆							◆	◆	◆
Patterns and Shapes										
Math Problem of the Day 56	◆	◆	◆				◆	◆	◆	◆
Math Problem of the Day 57		◆	◆				◆	◆	◆	◆
Math Problem of the Day 58	◆	◆					◆	◆	◆	◆
Math Problem of the Day 59		◆	◆				◆	◆	◆	◆
Math Problem of the Day 60		◆	◆				◆	◆	◆	◆
Math Problem of the Day 61	◆	◆					◆	◆	◆	◆
Math Problem of the Day 62	◆	◆					◆	◆	◆	◆
Math Problem of the Day 63	◆	◆					◆	◆	◆	◆
Math Problem of the Day 64	◆	◆					◆	◆	◆	◆
Math Problem of the Day 65		◆					◆	◆	◆	◆
Math Problem of the Day 66		◆	◆				◆	◆	◆	◆
Math Problem of the Day 67	◆	◆	◆				◆	◆	◆	◆
Math Problem of the Day 68	◆		◆			◆	◆	◆		◆
Math Problem of the Day 69			◆			◆		◆	◆	◆
Math Problem of the Day 70			◆			◆		◆	◆	◆
Math Problem of the Day 71			◆					◆		
Math Problem of the Day 72			◆					◆		
Math Problem of the Day 73			◆					◆	◆	
Math Problem of the Day 74			◆					◆	◆	
Math Problem of the Day 75	◆		◆				◆		◆	
Math Problem of the Day 76	◆		◆				◆		◆	
Math Problem of the Day 77	◆		◆				◆		◆	
Math Problem of the Day 78			◆					◆		
Math Problem of the Day 79			◆					◆	◆	◆
Math Problem of the Day 80	◆		◆			◆	◆	◆	◆	◆
Math Problem of the Day 81	◆		◆			◆	◆	◆	◆	◆
Math Problem of the Day 82	◆		◆			◆	◆	◆	◆	◆
Math Problem of the Day 83	◆		◆			◆	◆	◆	◆	◆
Math Problem of the Day 84	◆		◆			◆	◆	◆	◆	◆
Math Problem of the Day 85	◆		◆			◆	◆	◆	◆	◆
Math Problem of the Day 86	◆		◆				◆	◆	◆	◆
Math Problem of the Day 87			◆			◆	◆	◆	◆	◆
Math Problem of the Day 88			◆			◆	◆	◆	◆	◆
Math Problem of the Day 89			◆			◆	◆	◆	◆	◆
Math Problem of the Day 90			◆			◆	◆	◆	◆	◆
Map Skills and Location										
Math Problem of the Day 91			◆			◆		◆	◆	◆
Math Problem of the Day 92			◆			◆		◆	◆	◆
Math Problem of the Day 93			◆			◆		◆	◆	◆

Connections With the NCTM Standards

	Content Standards					Process Standards				
	Number and Operation	Patterns, Functions, and Algebra	Geometry and Spatial Sense	Measurement	Data Analysis, Statistics, and Probability	Problem Solving	Reasoning and Proof	Communication	Connections	Representation
Math Problem of the Day 94			◆			◆		◆	◆	◆
Math Problem of the Day 95			◆			◆		◆	◆	◆
Math Problem of the Day 96	◆		◆			◆				
Math Problem of the Day 97	◆		◆			◆				
Math Problem of the Day 98	◆		◆			◆				
Math Problem of the Day 99	◆		◆			◆				
Math Problem of the Day 100	◆		◆			◆				
Word Problems										
Math Problem of the Day 101	◆							◆	◆	◆
Math Problem of the Day 102	◆							◆	◆	◆
Math Problem of the Day 103	◆							◆	◆	◆
Math Problem of the Day 104	◆							◆	◆	◆
Math Problem of the Day 105	◆							◆	◆	◆
Math Problem of the Day 106	◆							◆	◆	◆
Math Problem of the Day 107	◆							◆	◆	◆
Math Problem of the Day 108	◆							◆	◆	◆
Math Problem of the Day 109			◆	◆			◆	◆	◆	◆
Math Problem of the Day 110				◆			◆	◆	◆	◆
Math Problem of the Day 111				◆			◆	◆	◆	◆
Math Problem of the Day 112	◆					◆		◆	◆	◆
Math Problem of the Day 113	◆					◆		◆	◆	◆
Math Problem of the Day 114	◆					◆		◆	◆	◆
Math Problem of the Day 115	◆					◆		◆	◆	◆
Measurement										
Math Problem of the Day 116				◆				◆	◆	◆
Math Problem of the Day 117				◆				◆	◆	◆
Math Problem of the Day 118				◆				◆	◆	◆
Math Problem of the Day 119				◆				◆	◆	
Math Problem of the Day 120				◆				◆	◆	
Math Problem of the Day 121				◆		◆		◆	◆	◆
Math Problem of the Day 122				◆		◆		◆	◆	◆
Math Problem of the Day 123				◆		◆		◆	◆	◆
Math Problem of the Day 124				◆		◆		◆	◆	◆
Math Problem of the Day 125				◆		◆		◆	◆	◆
Money										
Math Problem of the Day 126	◆			◆		◆				
Math Problem of the Day 127	◆			◆		◆				
Math Problem of the Day 128	◆			◆		◆				
Math Problem of the Day 129	◆			◆		◆				
Math Problem of the Day 130	◆			◆		◆				
Charts, Graphs, and Diagrams										
Math Problem of the Day 131	◆				◆			◆		◆
Math Problem of the Day 132	◆				◆			◆		◆
Math Problem of the Day 133	◆				◆			◆		◆
Math Problem of the Day 134	◆				◆			◆		◆
Math Problem of the Day 135	◆				◆			◆		◆
Math Problem of the Day 136	◆				◆			◆		◆
Math Problem of the Day 137	◆				◆			◆		◆

	Content Standards					Process Standards				
	Number and Operation	Patterns, Functions, and Algebra	Geometry and Spatial Sense	Measurement	Data Analysis, Statistics, and Probability	Problem Solving	Reasoning and Proof	Communication	Connections	Representation
Math Problem of the Day 138	◆				◆			◆		◆
Math Problem of the Day 139	◆				◆			◆		◆
Math Problem of the Day 140	◆				◆			◆		◆
Math Problem of the Day 141	◆				◆			◆		◆
Math Problem of the Day 142	◆				◆			◆		◆
Math Problem of the Day 143	◆				◆		◆	◆	◆	◆
Math Problem of the Day 144	◆				◆			◆	◆	◆
Math Problem of the Day 145	◆				◆			◆	◆	◆
Math Problem of the Day 146	◆				◆			◆	◆	◆
Math Problem of the Day 147	◆				◆			◆	◆	◆
Math Problem of the Day 148	◆	◆			◆	◆		◆	◆	◆
Math Problem of the Day 149	◆				◆			◆	◆	◆
Math Problem of the Day 150	◆				◆			◆	◆	◆
Math Problem of the Day 151	◆				◆	◆		◆	◆	◆
Math Problem of the Day 152	◆				◆			◆	◆	◆
Math Problem of the Day 153	◆				◆	◆		◆	◆	◆
Math Problem of the Day 154	◆				◆	◆		◆	◆	◆
Math Problem of the Day 155	◆				◆			◆	◆	◆
Math Problem of the Day 156	◆				◆	◆	◆	◆	◆	◆
Math Problem of the Day 157	◆				◆			◆		◆
Math Problem of the Day 158	◆				◆			◆		◆
Math Problem of the Day 159	◆				◆			◆		◆
Math Problem of the Day 160	◆				◆			◆		◆
Math Problem of the Day 161	◆				◆			◆		◆
Fractions										
Math Problem of the Day 162	◆		◆			◆				
Math Problem of the Day 163	◆		◆			◆				
Problem Solving										
Math Problem of the Day 164	◆				◆	◆	◆	◆		
Math Problem of the Day 165	◆				◆	◆	◆	◆		
Math Problem of the Day 166	◆				◆	◆	◆	◆		
Math Problem of the Day 167	◆				◆	◆	◆	◆		
Math Problem of the Day 168	◆				◆	◆	◆	◆		
Math Problem of the Day 169	◆				◆		◆	◆		
Math Problem of the Day 170	◆				◆		◆	◆		
Math Problem of the Day 171	◆				◆		◆	◆		
Math Problem of the Day 172	◆				◆		◆	◆		
Math Problem of the Day 173	◆				◆		◆	◆		
Math Problem of the Day 174	◆				◆	◆		◆	◆	◆
Math Problem of the Day 175	◆				◆	◆		◆	◆	◆
Math Problem of the Day 176	◆				◆			◆	◆	◆
Math Problem of the Day 177	◆				◆			◆	◆	◆
Math Problem of the Day 178				◆	◆	◆		◆	◆	◆
Math Problem of the Day 179				◆	◆	◆		◆	◆	◆
Math Problem of the Day 180				◆	◆	◆		◆	◆	◆

National Council of Teachers of Mathematics. (2000). *Principles and Standards for School Mathematics*. Reston, VA: NCTM. www.nctm.org

Name _____

Math Problem of the Day

Write the addition sentence.

1. _____ + _____ = _____

2. _____ + _____ = _____

Quick Review

How many?

1. _____

2. _____

Name _____

Math Problem of the Day

Write the addition sentence.

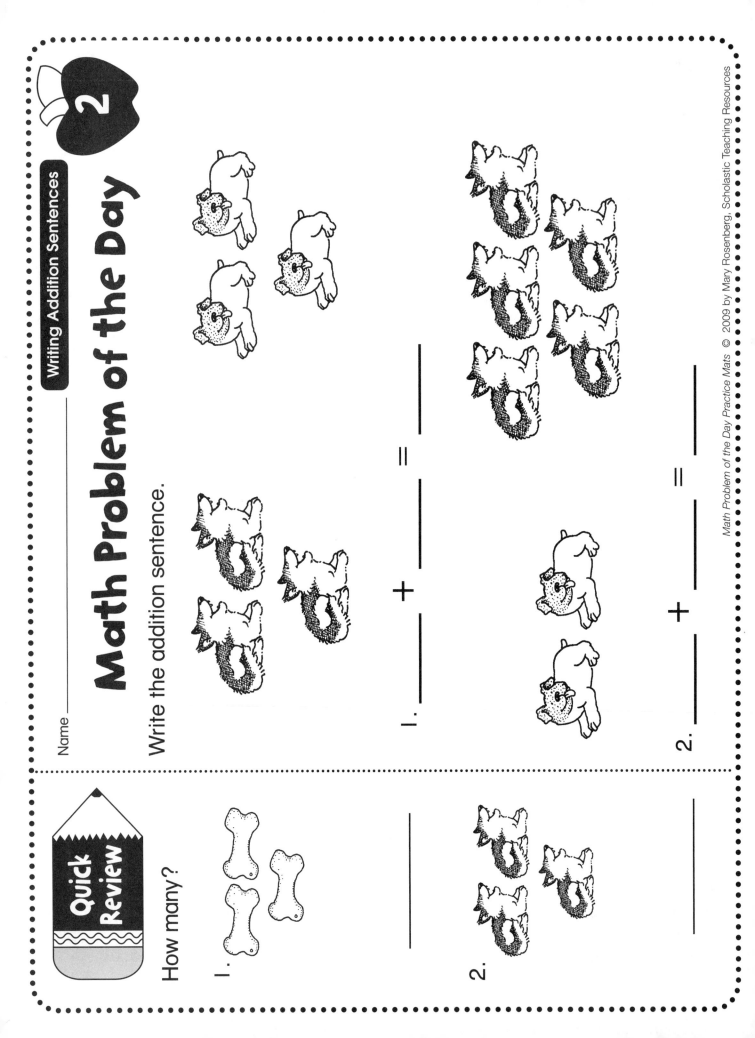

1. _____ + _____ = _____

2. _____ + _____ = _____

How many?

1. _____

2. _____

Math Problem of the Day

Name _____

Write the addition sentence.

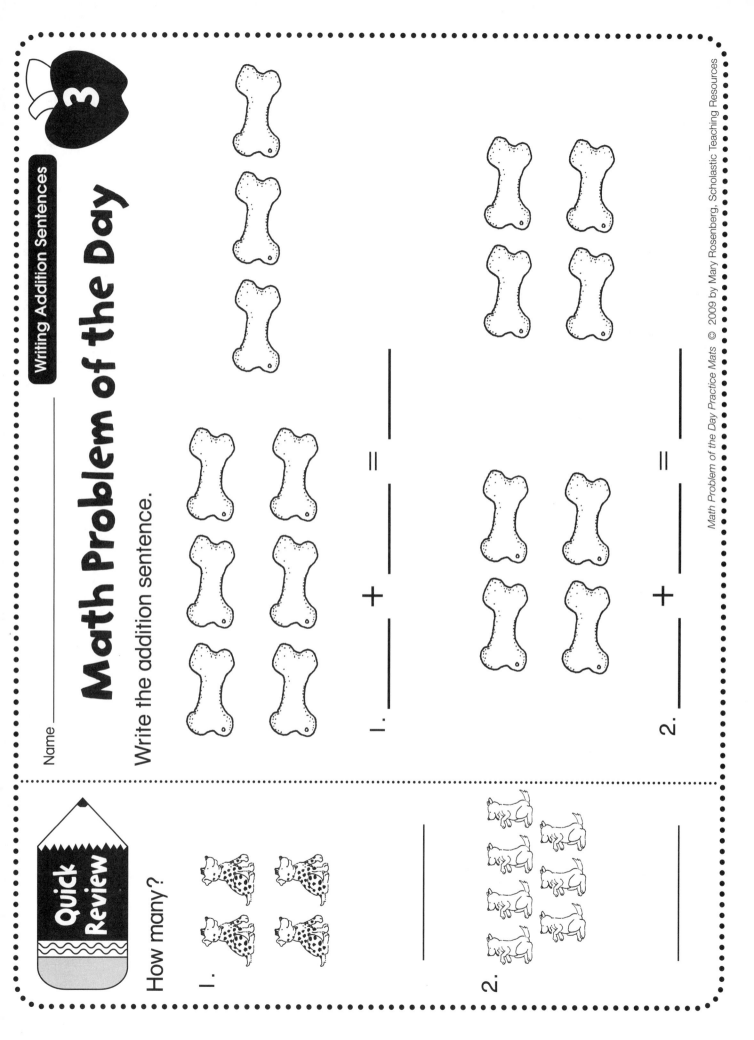

1. ____ + ____ = ____

2. ____ + ____ = ____

Quick Review

How many?

1. ____

2. ____

Name _____

Math Problem of the Day

4

Write the addition sentence.

1. _____ + _____ = _____

2. _____ + _____ = _____

Quick Review

How many?

1. _____

2. _____

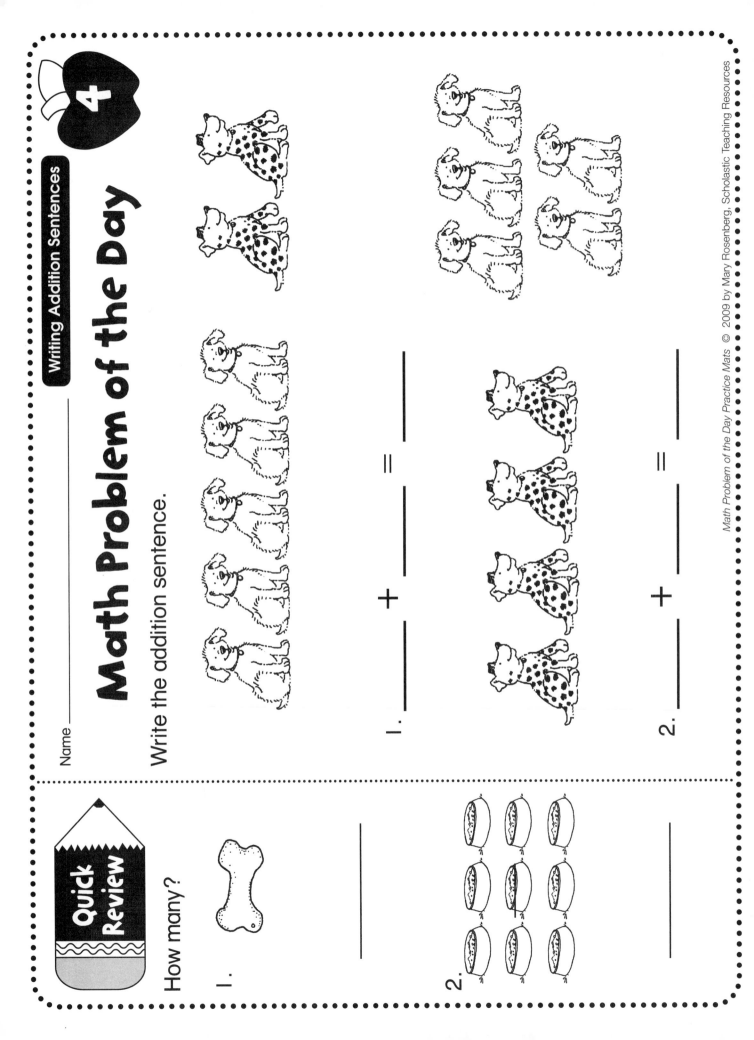

Math Problem of the Day

Name _____

Write the addition sentence.

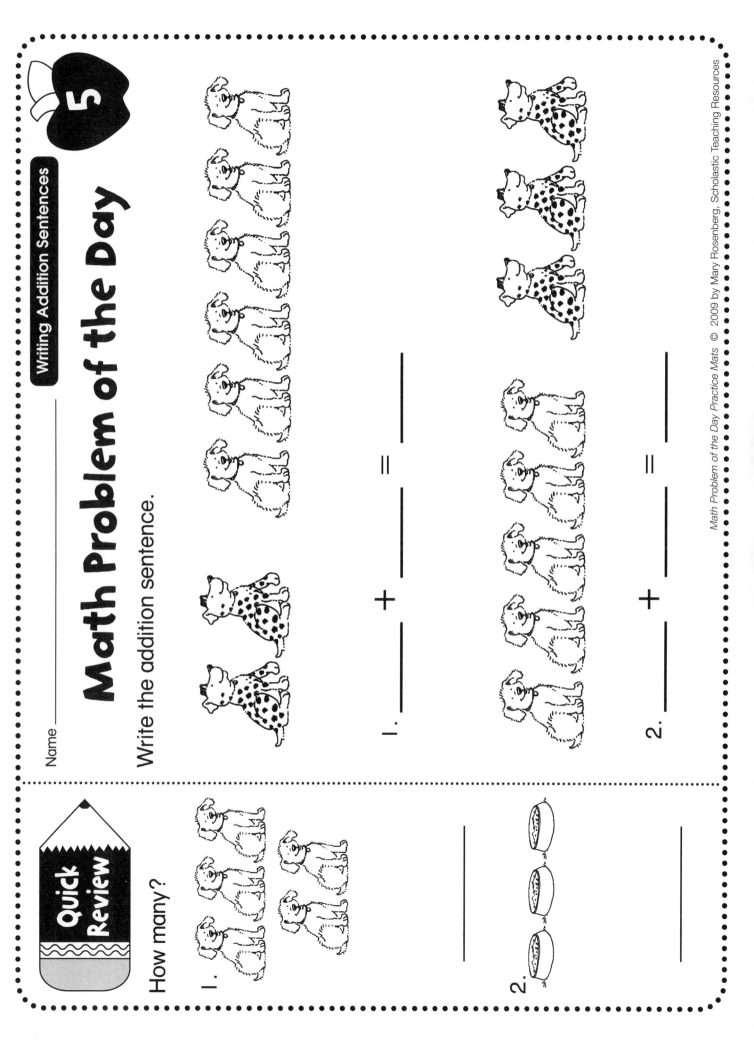

1. ___ + ___ = ___

2. ___ + ___ = ___

Quick Review

How many?

1. ___

2. ___

Name _____

Math Problem of the Day

Use the number line to solve each problem.

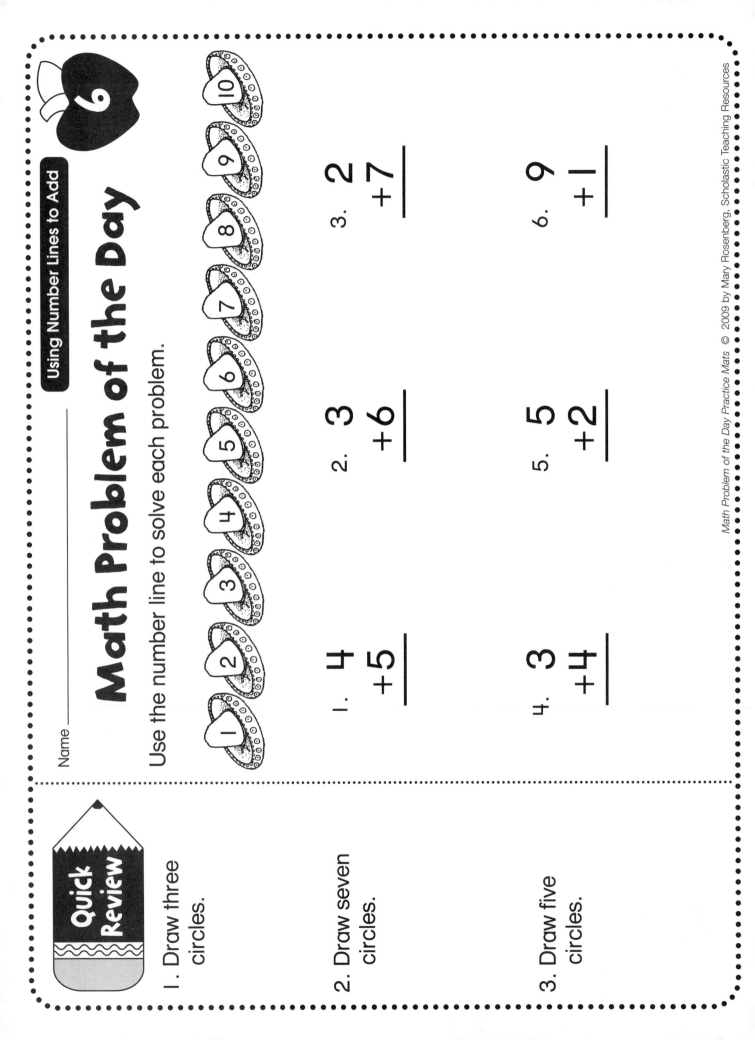

1 2 3 4 5 6 7 8 9 10

1. 4
   +5
   ___

2. 3
   +6
   ___

3. 2
   +7
   ___

4. 3
   +4
   ___

5. 5
   +2
   ___

6. 9
   +1
   ___

Math Problem of the Day Practice Mats © 2009 by Mary Rosenberg, Scholastic Teaching Resources

Quick Review

1. Draw three circles.

2. Draw seven circles.

3. Draw five circles.

Name _____

Math Problem of the Day

Use the number line to solve each problem.

1 (2) 3 (4) 5 (6) 7 (8) 9 (10)

1. $\begin{array}{r} 6 \\ +2 \\ \hline \end{array}$

2. $\begin{array}{r} 8 \\ +1 \\ \hline \end{array}$

3. $\begin{array}{r} 5 \\ +3 \\ \hline \end{array}$

4. $\begin{array}{r} 3 \\ +7 \\ \hline \end{array}$

5. $\begin{array}{r} 6 \\ +4 \\ \hline \end{array}$

6. $\begin{array}{r} 2 \\ +2 \\ \hline \end{array}$

Quick Review

1. Draw two squares.

2. Draw eight squares.

3. Draw four squares.

Name _____

Math Problem of the Day

Use the number line to solve each problem.

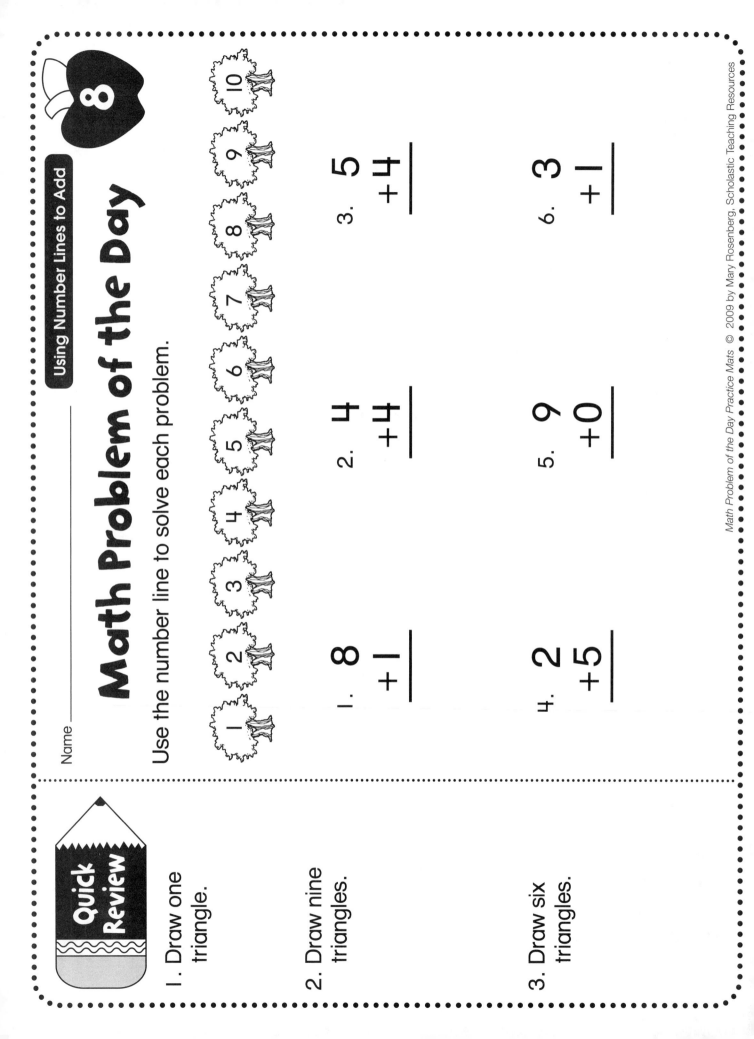

1   2   3   4   5   6   7   8   9   10

1. 8
   +1
   ———

2. 4
   +4
   ———

3. 5
   +4
   ———

4. 2
   +5
   ———

5. 9
   +0
   ———

6. 3
   +1
   ———

Quick Review

1. Draw one triangle.

2. Draw nine triangles.

3. Draw six triangles.

Name _____

Math Problem of the Day

Use the number line to solve each problem.

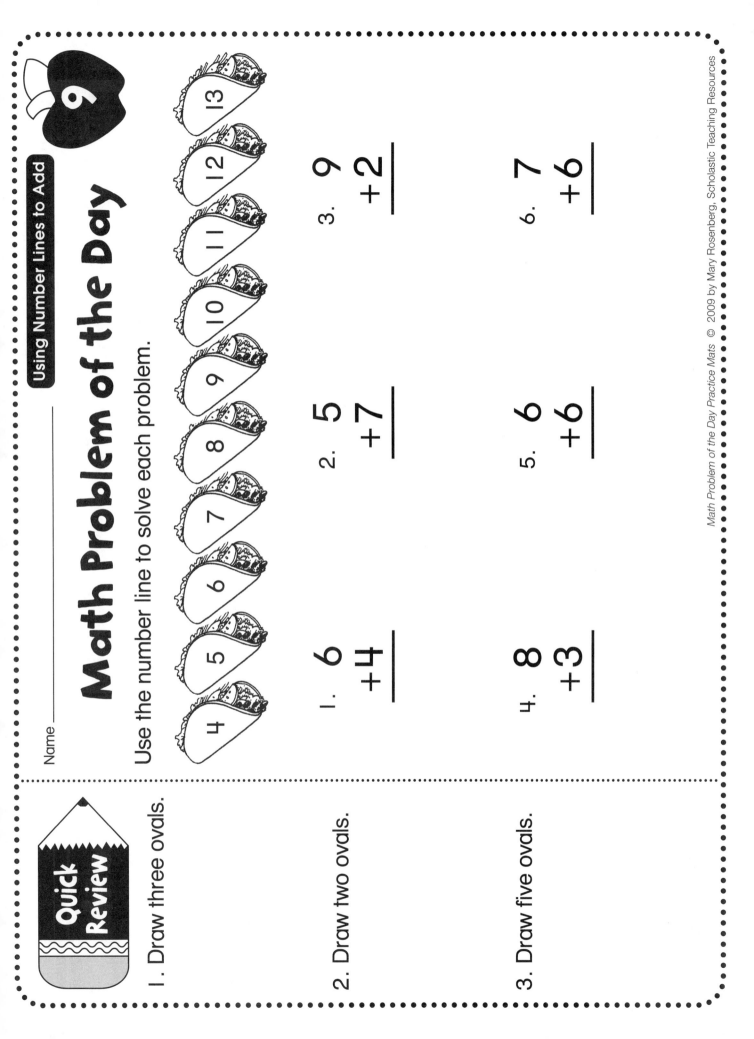

4   5   6   7   8   9   10   11   12   13

1.   6
    +4
    ‾‾‾

2.   5
    +7
    ‾‾‾

3.   9
    +2
    ‾‾‾

4.   8
    +3
    ‾‾‾

5.   6
    +6
    ‾‾‾

6.   7
    +6
    ‾‾‾

Quick Review

1. Draw three ovals.

2. Draw two ovals.

3. Draw five ovals.

Math Problem of the Day Practice Mats © 2009 by Mary Rosenberg, Scholastic Teaching Resources

Math Problem of the Day Practice Mats © 2009 by Mary Rosenberg, Scholastic Teaching Resources

Math Problem of the Day

Name _____

Use number line to solve each problem.

| 6 | 7 | 8 | 9 | 10 | 11 | 12 | 13 | 14 | 15 |

1. 7
   +7
   ___

2. 8
   +5
   ___

3. 7
   +8
   ___

4. 9
   +3
   ___

5. 6
   +7
   ___

6. 9
   +6
   ___

Quick Review

1. Draw four rectangles.

2. Draw six rectangles.

3. Draw seven rectangles.

11

Name _____

Math Problem of the Day

Draw a picture to solve the problem.

Write the number sentence on the line.

Syd planted one apple tree and three orange trees.

How many trees did Syd plant?

_____

Quick Review

1. Color 3 apples.

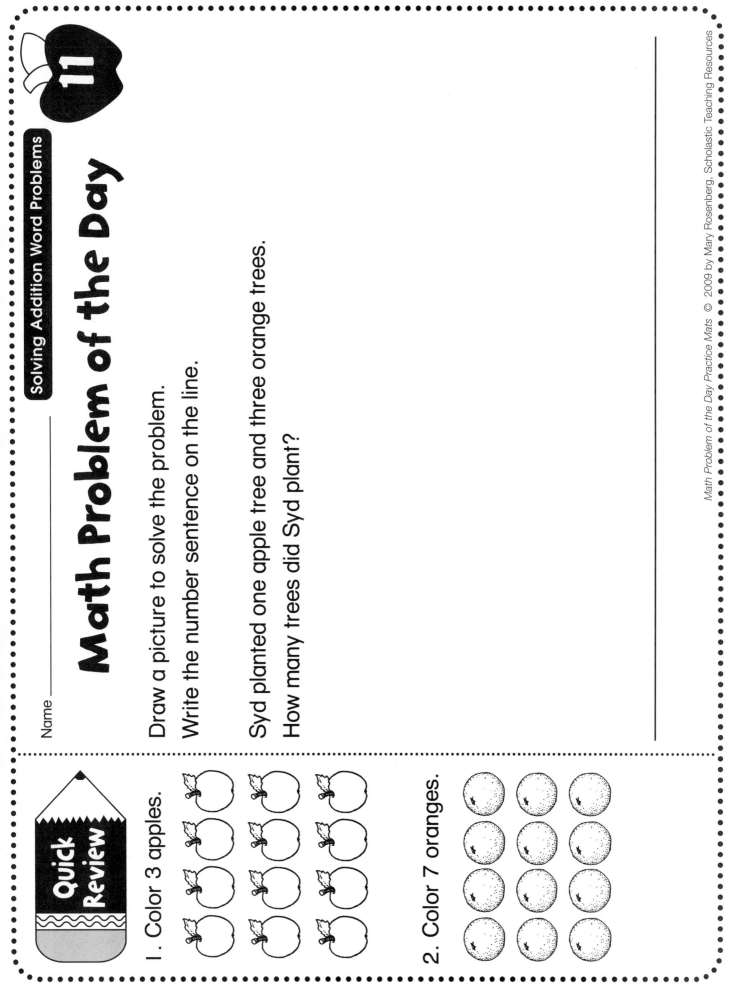

2. Color 7 oranges.

12

Math Problem of the Day

Name _____

Draw a picture to solve the problem.

Write the number sentence on the line.

Dennis planted two apple seeds and seven pumpkin seeds.

How many seeds did Dennis plant in all?

_____

Quick Review

1. Color 8 apples.

2. Color 5 pumpkins.

13

Name _____

Math Problem of the Day

Draw a picture to solve the problem.
Write the number sentence on the line.

Lori picked up four acorns.

Then she picked up three more acorns.

How many acorns does Lori have?

Quick Review

1. Color 9 acorns.

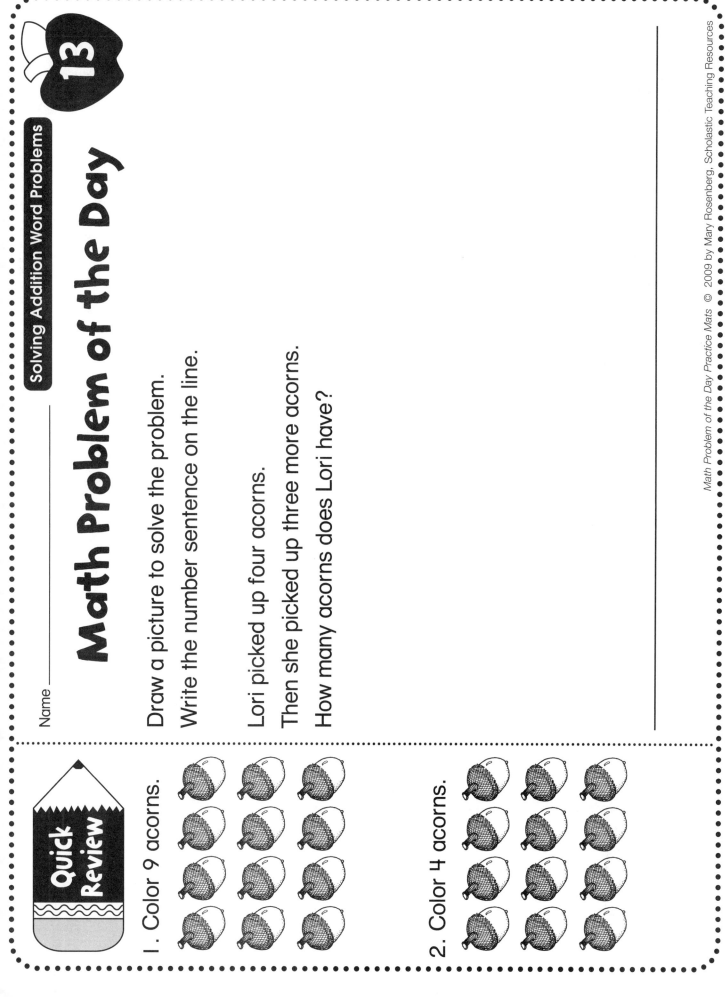

2. Color 4 acorns.

Solving Addition Word Problems

Math Problem of the Day

Name _____

Draw a picture to solve the problem.
Write the number sentence on the line.

Sam picked five pears for his mom.
He picked three pears for his dad.
How many pears did Sam pick?

_____

Quick Review

1. Color 10 pears.

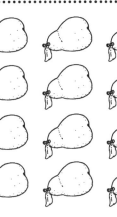

2. Color 2 pears.

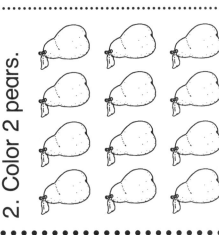

Name _____

Math Problem of the Day

Draw a picture to solve the problem.
Write the number sentence on the line.

Ciera ate three large strawberries.

Then she ate six small strawberries.

How many strawberries did Ciera eat?

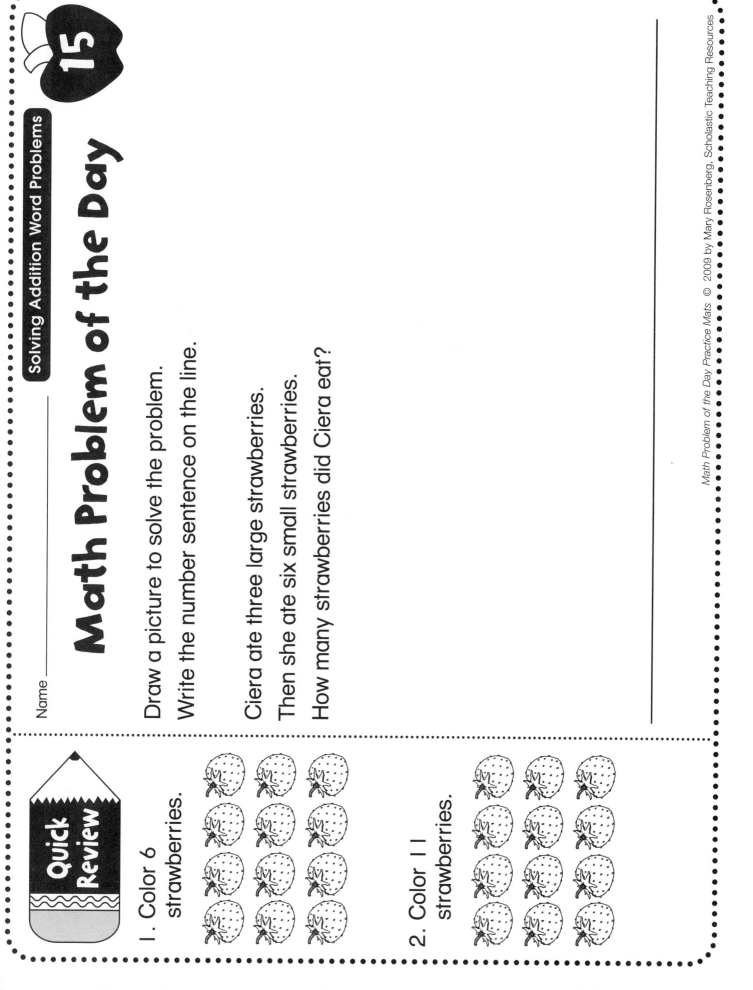

Quick Review

1. Color 6 strawberries.

2. Color 11 strawberries.

Math Problem of the Day Practice Mats © 2009 by Mary Rosenberg, Scholastic Teaching Resources

Name _____

Writing Subtraction Sentences

Math Problem of the Day

Write the subtraction problem.

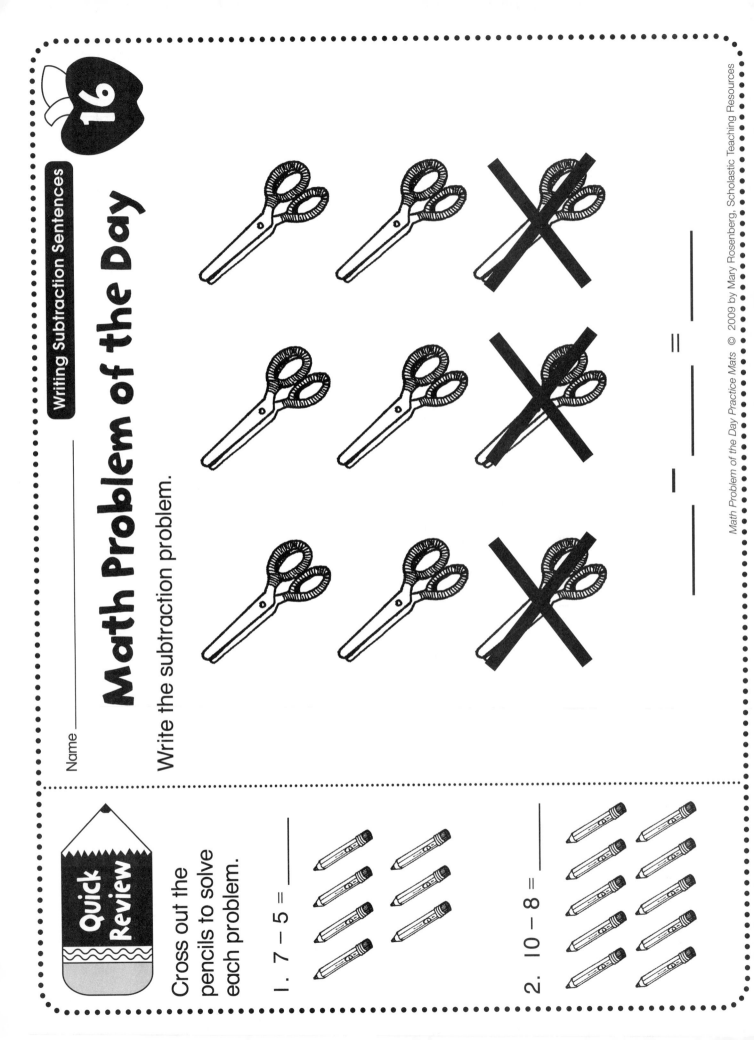

_____ − _____ = _____

Quick Review

Cross out the pencils to solve each problem.

1. 7 − 5 = _____

2. 10 − 8 = _____

Math Problem of the Day

Name _____

Write the subtraction problem.

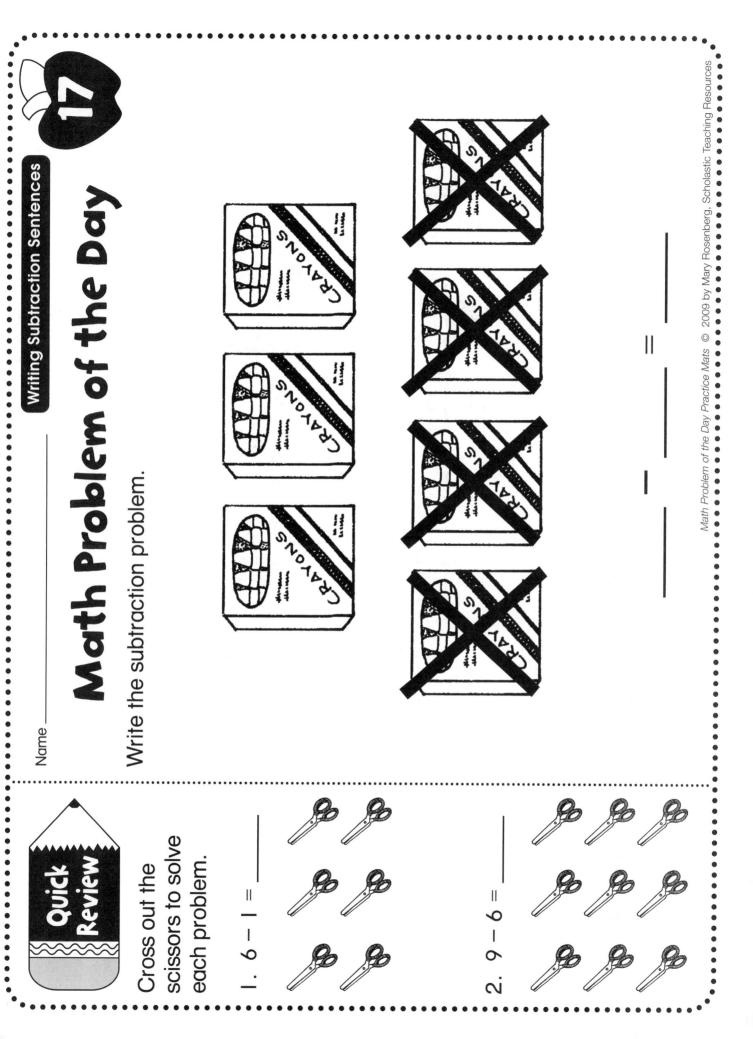

___ ___ = ___

Quick Review

Cross out the scissors to solve each problem.

1. 6 – 1 = _____

2. 9 – 6 = _____

Name _____

Math Problem of the Day

Write the subtraction problem.

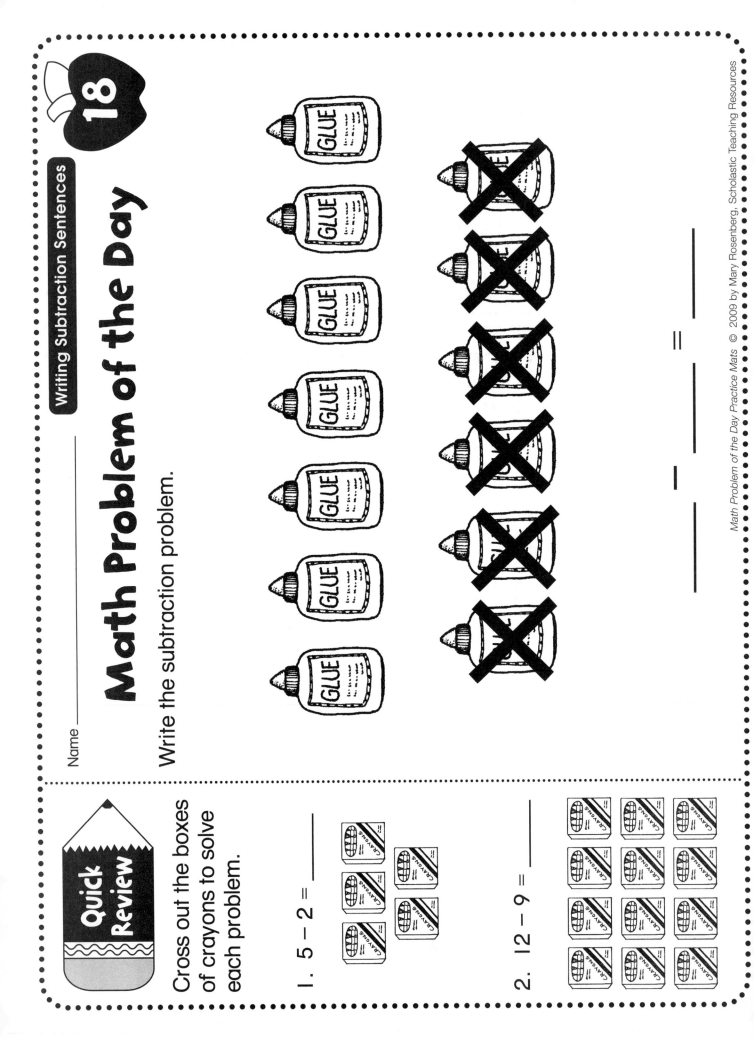

_____ — _____ = _____

Math Problem of the Day Practice Mats © 2009 by Mary Rosenberg, Scholastic Teaching Resources

Quick Review

Cross out the boxes of crayons to solve each problem.

1. 5 – 2 = _____

2. 12 – 9 = _____

Name _____

Math Problem of the Day

Write the subtraction problem.

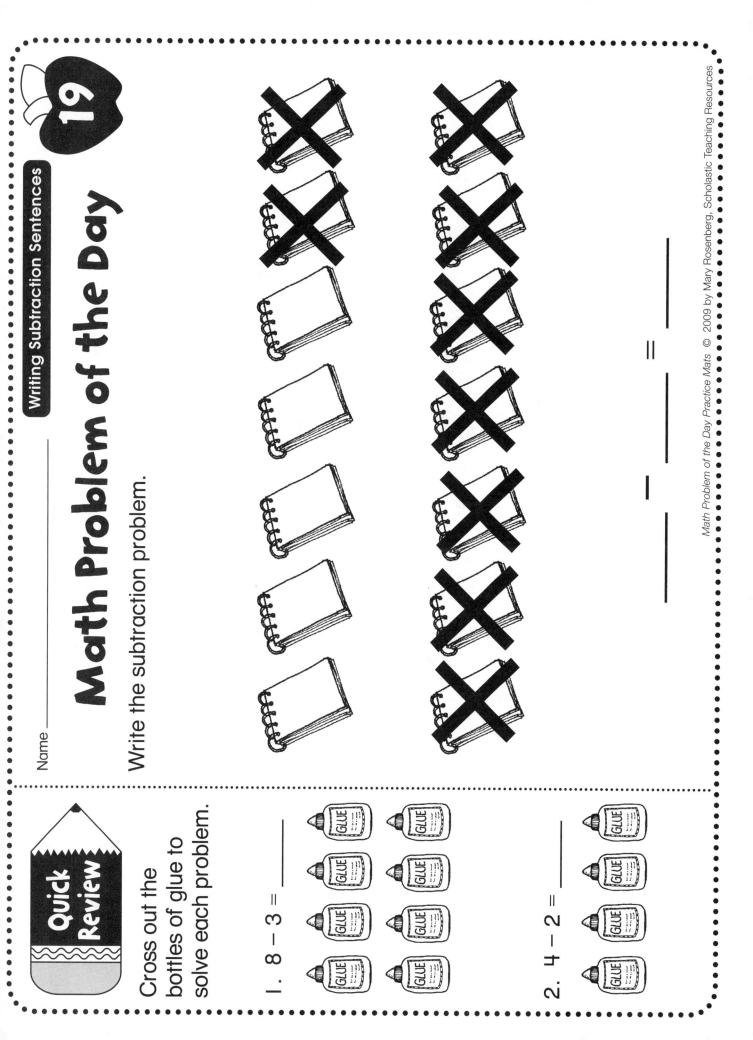

___ − ___ = ___

Quick Review

Cross out the bottles of glue to solve each problem.

1. $8 - 3 = $ ___

2. $4 - 2 = $ ___

Writing Subtraction Sentences

Math Problem of the Day

Name _____

Write the subtraction problem.

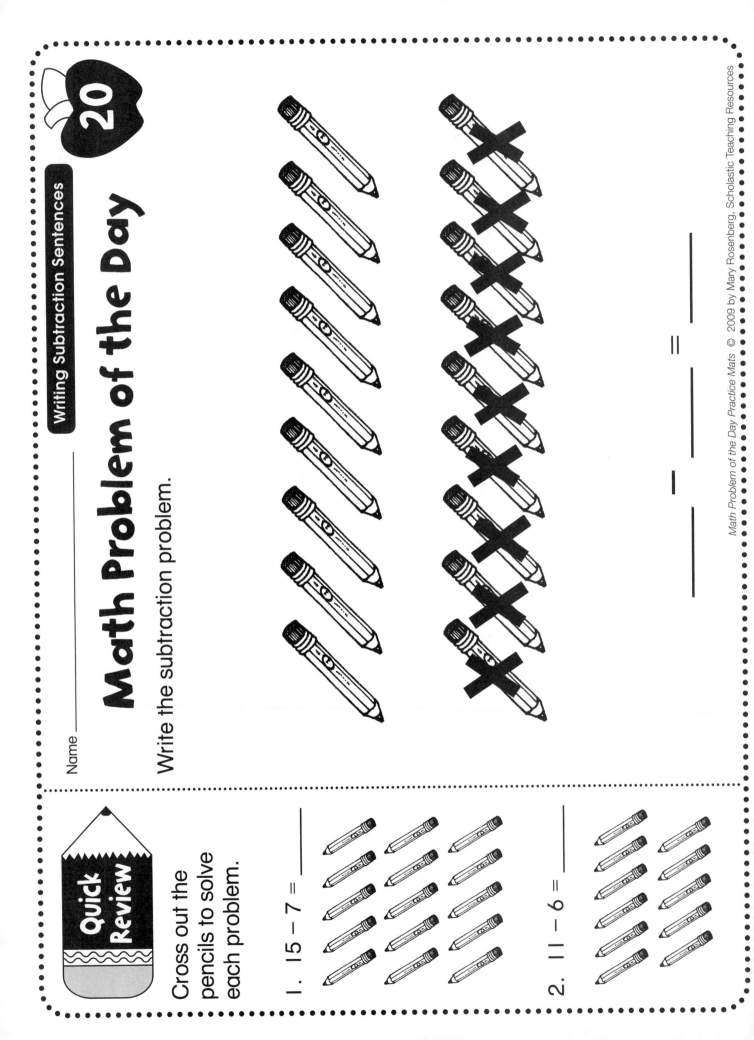

___ − ___ = ___

Math Problem of the Day Practice Mats © 2009 by Mary Rosenberg, Scholastic Teaching Resources

Quick Review

Cross out the pencils to solve each problem.

1. 15 − 7 = ___

2. 11 − 6 = ___

Name _____

Math Problem of the Day

Using Number Lines to Subtract

Use the number line to solve each problem.

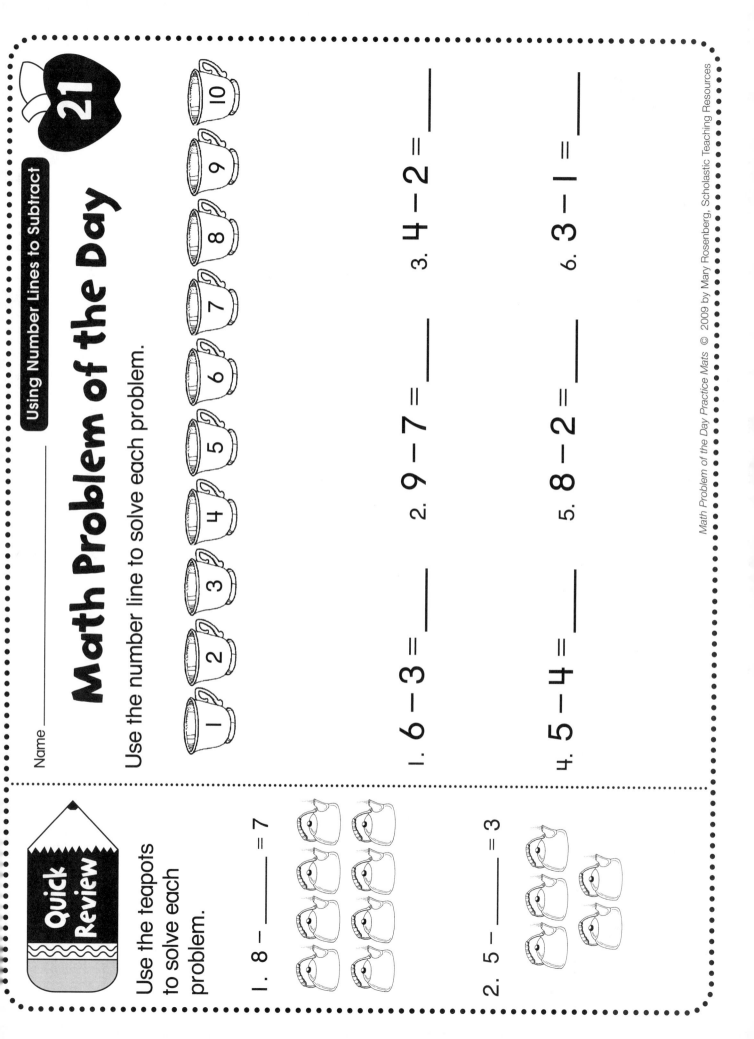

| 1 | 2 | 3 | 4 | 5 | 6 | 7 | 8 | 9 | 10 |

1. 6 – 3 = _____

2. 9 – 7 = _____

3. 4 – 2 = _____

4. 5 – 4 = _____

5. 8 – 2 = _____

6. 3 – 1 = _____

Quick Review

Use the teapots to solve each problem.

1. 8 – _____ = 7

2. 5 – _____ = 3

Math Problem of the Day Practice Mats © 2009 by Mary Rosenberg, Scholastic Teaching Resources

Math Problem of the Day

Name _____

Use the number line to solve each problem.

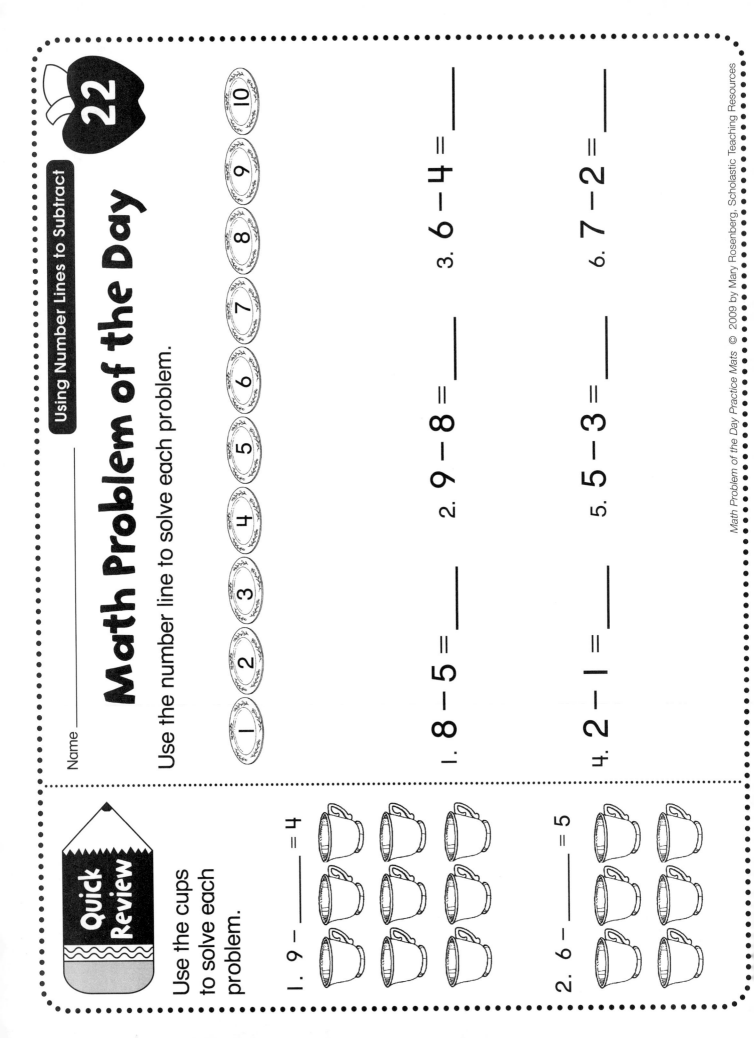

$$1 \quad 2 \quad 3 \quad 4 \quad 5 \quad 6 \quad 7 \quad 8 \quad 9 \quad 10$$

1. $8 - 5 =$ _____

2. $9 - 8 =$ _____

3. $6 - 4 =$ _____

4. $2 - 1 =$ _____

5. $5 - 3 =$ _____

6. $7 - 2 =$ _____

Quick Review

Use the cups to solve each problem.

1. $9 -$ _____ $= 4$

2. $6 -$ _____ $= 5$

Name _____

Math Problem of the Day

Use the number line to solve each problem.

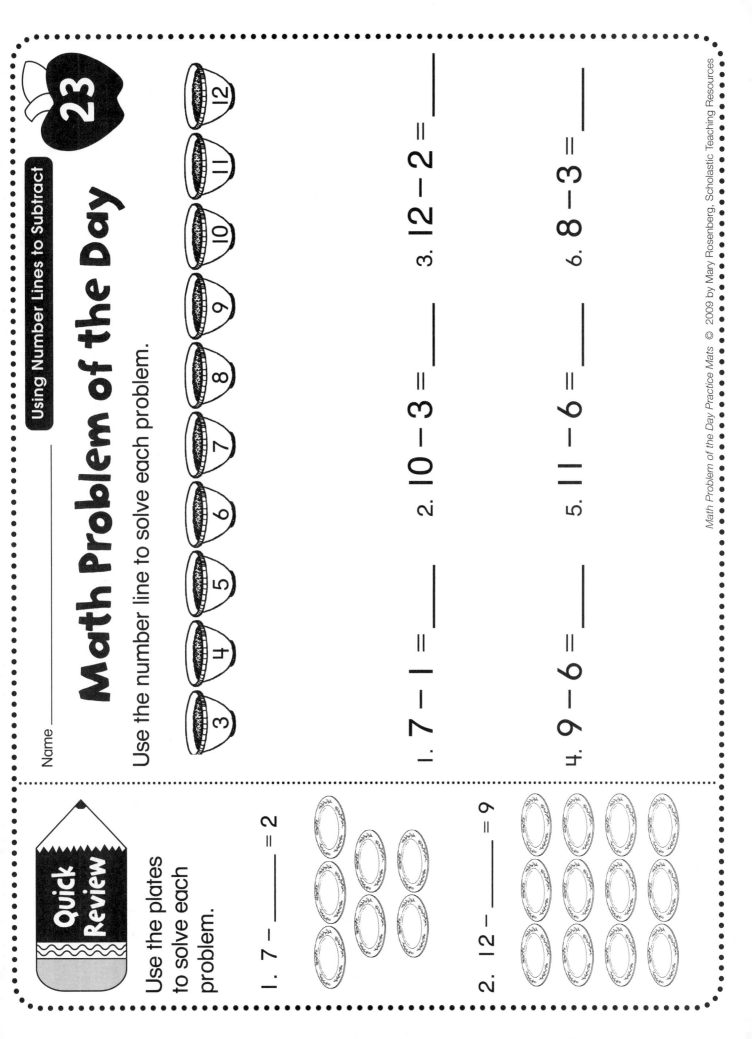

3 4 5 6 7 8 9 10 11 12

1. 7 − 1 = _____

2. 10 − 3 = _____

3. 12 − 2 = _____

4. 9 − 6 = _____

5. 11 − 6 = _____

6. 8 − 3 = _____

Quick Review

Use the plates to solve each problem.

1. 7 − _____ = 2

2. 12 − _____ = 9

Math Problem of the Day

Name _____

Use the number line to solve each problem.

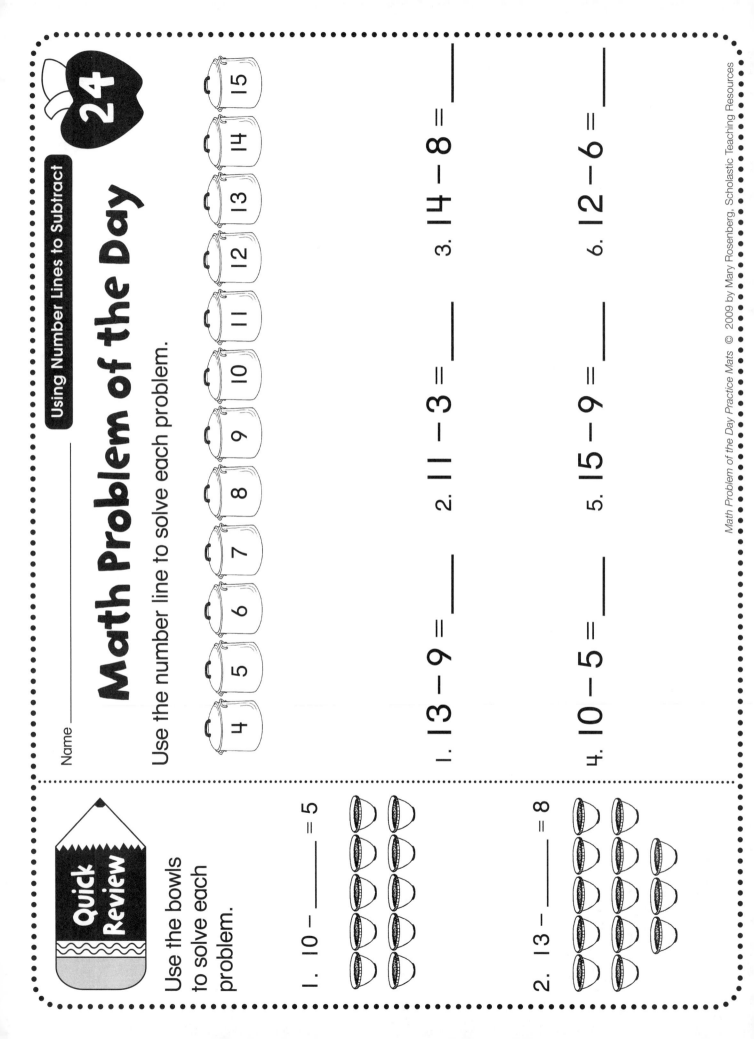

4 5 6 7 8 9 10 11 12 13 14 15

1. $13 - 9 =$ _____

2. $11 - 3 =$ _____

3. $14 - 8 =$ _____

4. $10 - 5 =$ _____

5. $15 - 9 =$ _____

6. $12 - 6 =$ _____

Quick Review

Use the bowls to solve each problem.

1. $10 -$ _____ $= 5$

2. $13 -$ _____ $= 8$

Name _____

Math Problem of the Day

Using Number Lines to Subtract

Use the number line to solve each problem.

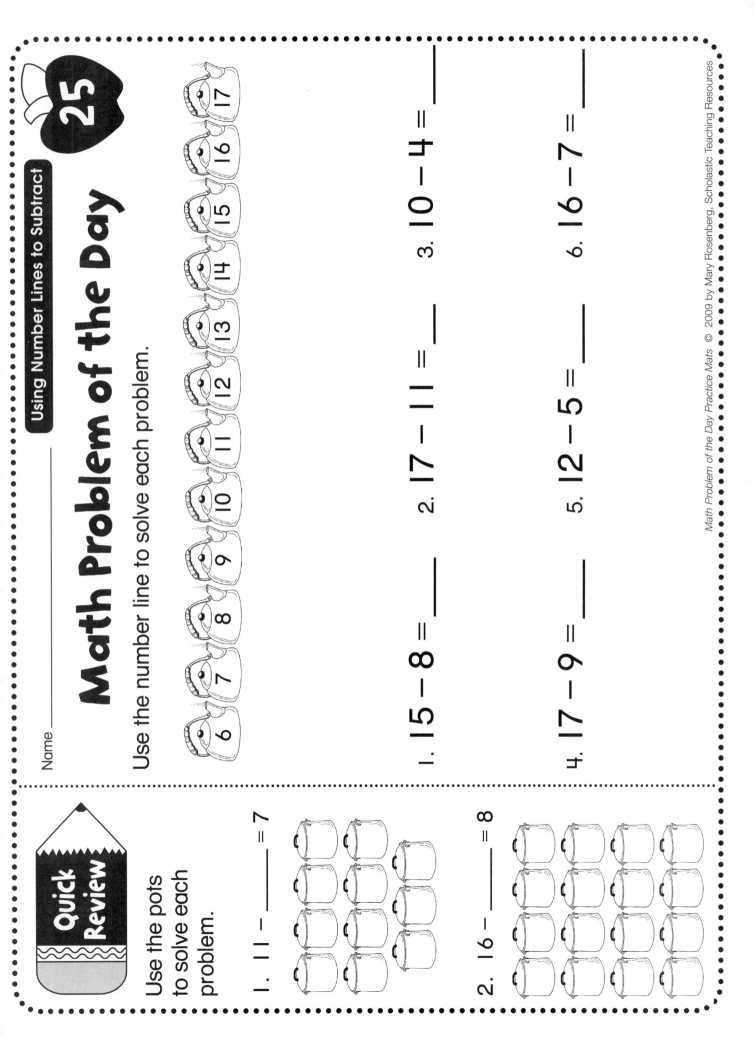

6 7 8 9 10 11 12 13 14 15 16 17

1. 15 − 8 = ____

2. 17 − 11 = ____

3. 10 − 4 = ____

4. 17 − 9 = ____

5. 12 − 5 = ____

6. 16 − 7 = ____

Quick Review

Use the pots to solve each problem.

1. 11 − ____ = 7

2. 16 − ____ = 8

Math Problem of the Day

Name _____

Draw a picture to solve the problem.
Write the number sentence on the line.

George made 10 cookies. Then he ate six cookies.
How many cookies does George have left?

_____

Quick Review

Count backwards.

1. 20, _____,
_____, 17

2. 13, _____, 11,
_____

3. 10, _____,
_____, 7

4. 5, _____, 3,
_____

Math Problem of the Day Practice Mats © 2009 by Mary Rosenberg, Scholastic Teaching Resources

Name _____

Math Problem of the Day

Solving Subtraction Word Problems

Draw a picture to solve the problem.

Write the number sentence on the line.

Lucy had six ice cream cones. She ate two of them.

How many ice cream cones are left?

_____

Quick Review

Count backwards.

1. 17, ____, 15, ____

2. 13, 12, ____, ____

3. 19, ____, 17, ____

4. 14, 13, ____, ____

Solving Subtraction Word Problems

Math Problem of the Day

Name _____

Draw a picture to solve the problem.
Write the number sentence on the line.

Benny poured eight cups of milk. He gave three cups to his friends.

How many cups of milk does Benny have left?

_____

Quick Review

Count backwards.

1. 4, 3, _____, _____

2. 8, _____, _____, 5

3. 11, _____, 9, _____

4. 16, _____, _____, 13

Solving Subtraction Word Problems

Math Problem of the Day

Name _____

Draw a picture to solve the problem.
Write the number sentence on the line.

Caroline had nine grapes. She ate two grapes.
How many grapes does Caroline have left?

_____

Quick Review

Count backwards.

1. _____, 11,

_____, 9

2. _____, 16,

15, _____

3. _____, 19,

_____, 17

4. _____, 12,

_____, 10

Solving Subtraction Word Problems

Math Problem of the Day

Name _____

Draw a picture to solve the problem.

Write the number sentence on the line.

Thomas made seven cupcakes.

He gave four cupcakes to his friend.

How many cupcakes does Thomas have left?

_____

Math Problem of the Day Practice Mats © 2009 by Mary Rosenberg, Scholastic Teaching Resources

Quick Review

Count backwards.

1. ____ , ____ , 11, 10

2. ____ , ____ , 3, 2

3. ____ , ____ , 17, 16

4. ____ , ____ , 6, 5

Name _____

Math Problem of the Day

Compare the numbers. Use the number line.
Write > or < in each number sentence.

1 2 3 4 5 6 7 8 9 10

1. 9 ____ 4

2. 3 ____ 1

3. 6 ____ 8

4. 5 ____ 7

5. 4 ____ 2

6. 1 ____ 5

Quick Review

1. Color the 3rd apple.

2. Color the 1st apple.

3. Color the 2nd apple.

Name _____

Math Problem of the Day

Comparing Numbers

32

Compare the numbers. Use the number line.

Write > or < in each number sentence.

11 12 13 14 15 16 17 18 19 20

1. 11 _____ 18

2. 15 _____ 13

3. 16 _____ 19

4. 17 _____ 16

5. 14 _____ 11

6. 12 _____ 20

Quick Review

1. Color the 4th grape.

2. Color the 6th grape.

3. Color the 5th grape.

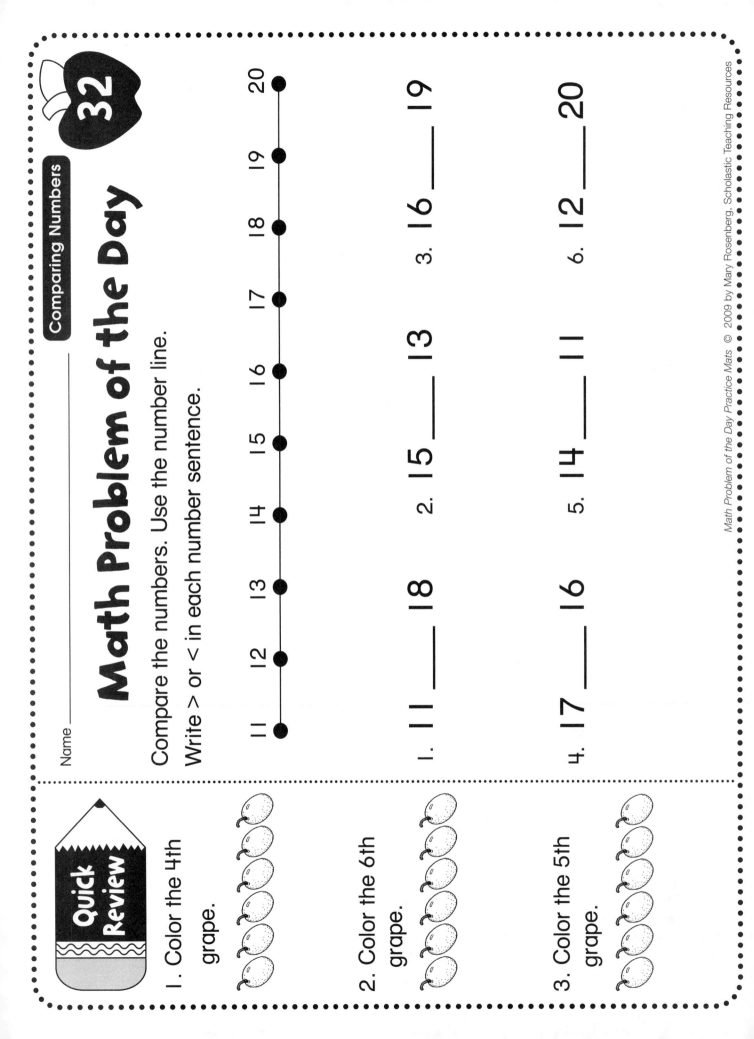

Name _____

Math Problem of the Day

Compare the numbers. Use the chart.

Write > or < in each number sentence.

21	22	23	24	25	26	27	28	29	30
31	32	33	34	35	36	37	38	39	40
41	42	43	44	45	46	47	48	49	50

1. 44 ___ 47

2. 37 ___ 47

3. 50 ___ 25

4. 40 ___ 31

5. 21 ___ 39

6. 36 ___ 23

Quick Review

Solve each problem.

1. 24 + 3 = ___

2. 33 + 6 = ___

3. 47 + 2 = ___

4. 28 + 1 = ___

Name _____

Math Problem of the Day

34

Compare the numbers. Use the chart.

Write > or < in each number sentence.

71	72	73	74	75	76	77	78	79	80
81	82	83	84	85	86	87	88	89	90
91	92	93	94	95	96	97	98	99	100

1. 83 ___ 91

2. 90 ___ 89

3. 72 ___ 99

4. 80 ___ 100

5. 97 ___ 79

6. 83 ___ 78

Quick Review

Solve each problem.

1. 82 + 6 = ___

2. 95 + 4 = ___

3. 72 + 7 = ___

4. 73 + 5 = ___

Identifying Even Numbers

Math Problem of the Day

Name _____

Circle the even numbers.

8

4

5

2

1

9

6

3

10

7

Put the even numbers in order.

____ , ____ , ____ , ____ , ____

Quick Review

Count by twos.
Write each
missing number.

1 . 2, _____, 6

2 . 6, _____, 10

3 . 4, 6, _____

4 . _____, 4, 6

Name _____

Math Problem of the Day

Draw an X on the odd numbers.

8   5   2

7   3   6   1

9   4

10

Put the odd numbers in order.

___ , ___ , ___ , ___ , ___

Quick Review

Write each
missing number.

1. 2, ___, 4, 5

2. 5, 6, ___, 8

3. ___, 2, ___, 4

4. 6, ___, 8, ___

Math Problem of the Day Practice Mats © 2009 by Mary Rosenberg, Scholastic Teaching Resources

Math Problem of the Day

Name _____

Circle the even numbers.

Draw an X on the odd numbers.

27   62   81

46

93   58

20   34   15

59

Quick Review

1. How many sets of two? _____

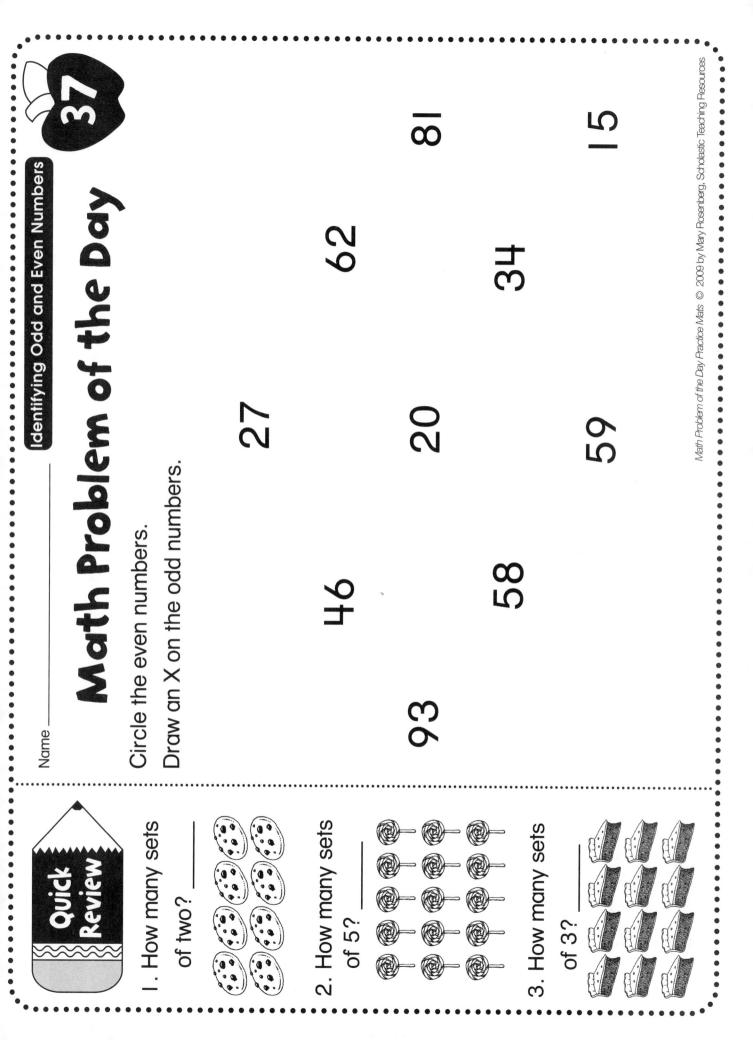

2. How many sets of 5? _____

3. How many sets of 3? _____

Name _____

Math Problem of the Day

Jack picked a mystery number.
Use the clues to guess it.

The number is:
• an odd number
• greater than 8
• less than 10

Circle Jack's mystery number.

I 2 3 4 5 6 7 8 9 10 11 12

Quick Review

Write the number.

1. three _____

2. six _____

3. nine _____

4. eight _____

5. two _____

Math Problem of the Day

Name _____

Rita picked a mystery number.
Use the clues to guess it.

The number is:

• an even number

• greater than 13

• less than 15

Circle Rita's mystery number.

3   4   5   6   7   8   9   10   11   12   13   14   15

Math Problem of the Day Practice Mats © 2009 by Mary Rosenberg, Scholastic Teaching Resources

Quick Review

Write the number.

1. seven _____

2. four _____

3. five _____

4. one _____

5. ten _____

Math Problem of the Day

Bruce picked a mystery number.
Use the chart and clues to find the number.

The number is:

- an even number
- less than 40
- greater than 36

Color Bruce's mystery number.

31	32	33	34	35	36	37	38	39	40
41	42	43	44	45	46	47	48	49	50
51	52	53	54	55	56	57	58	59	60

Quick Review

Compare the numbers. Write > or < on each line.

1. 38 _____ 48

2. 45 _____ 55

3. 59 _____ 33

4. 40 _____ 60

Using Deductive Reasoning

Math Problem of the Day

Name _____

Greta picked a mystery number.

Use the chart and clues to find the number.

The number is:
- an odd number
- greater than 71
- less than 75

Color Greta's mystery number.

61	62	63	64	65	66	67	68	69	70
71	72	73	74	75	76	77	78	79	80
81	82	83	84	85	86	87	88	89	90

Quick Review

Compare the numbers. Write > or < on each line.

1. 77 _____ 71

2. 62 _____ 82

3. 90 _____ 79

4. 88 _____ 89

Name _____

Math Problem of the Day

Walt picked a mystery number.

Use the chart and clues to find the number.

The number is:

• an odd number

• greater than 25

• less than 40

• made up of two digits that are the same

Color Walt's mystery number.

1	2	3	4	5	6	7	8	9	10
11	12	13	14	15	16	17	18	19	20
21	22	23	24	25	26	27	28	29	30
31	32	33	34	35	36	37	38	39	40
41	42	43	44	45	46	47	48	49	50

Math Problem of the Day Practice Mats © 2009 by Mary Rosenberg, Scholastic Teaching Resources

Quick Review

Write the number.

1. ten _____

2. eleven _____

3. twenty _____

4. twelve _____

5. fifty _____

Name _____

Math Problem of the Day

Betsy picked a mystery number.

Use the chart and clues to find the number.

The number is:

• an even number

• greater than 80

• used when counting by tens

• made up of two digits

Color Betsy's mystery number.

51	52	53	54	55	56	57	58	59	60
61	62	63	64	65	66	67	68	69	70
71	72	73	74	75	76	77	78	79	80
81	82	83	84	85	86	87	88	89	90
91	92	93	94	95	96	97	98	99	100

Quick Review

Write the number.

1. eighty _____

2. sixty _____

3. ninety _____

4. seventy _____

5. thirty _____

Math Problem of the Day

Circle sets of ten.

Write the number of tens and ones.

_____ tens _____ ones

What is the number? _____

Quick Review

Match each word to its number.

six   1

one   2

three   3

eight   6

two   8

Name _____

Math Problem of the Day

Circle sets of ten.

Write the number of tens and ones.

_____ tens _____ ones

What is the number? _____

Quick Review

Match each word to its number.

nine	3
three	4
seven	9
four	5
five	7

Math Problem of the Day Practice Mats © 2009 by Mary Rosenberg, Scholastic Teaching Resources

Identifying Sets

Name _____

Math Problem of the Day

Circle sets of ten.

Write the number of tens and ones.

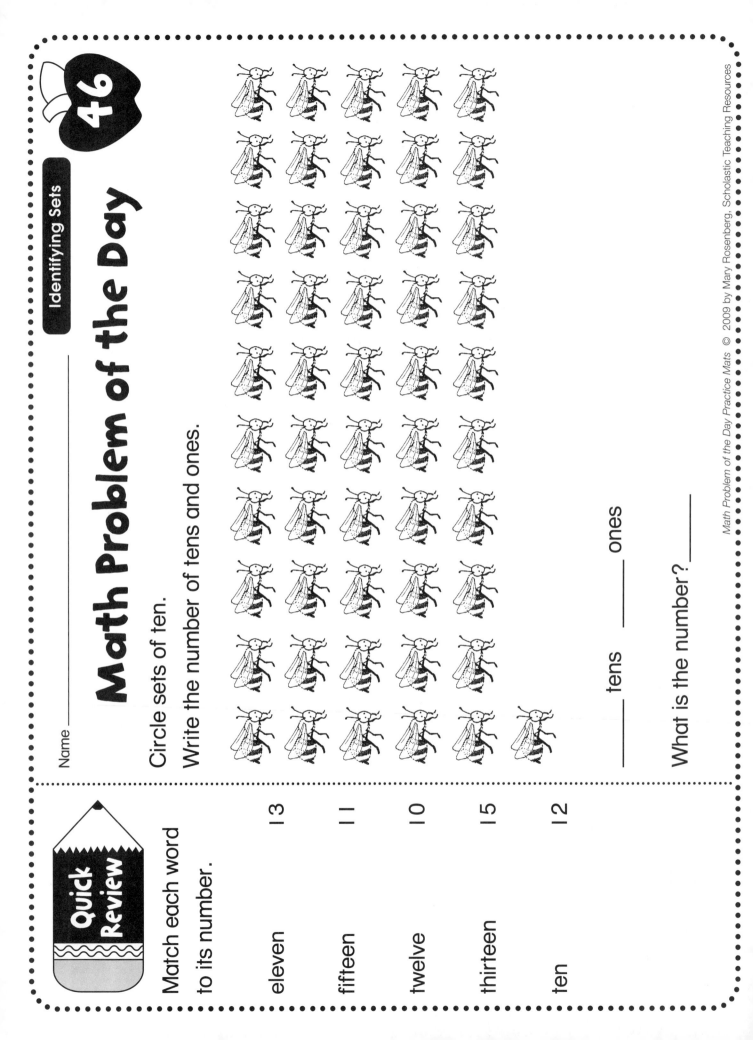

____ tens ____ ones

What is the number? _____

Quick Review

Match each word
to its number.

eleven   13

fifteen   11

twelve   10

thirteen   15

ten   12

Identifying Sets

Math Problem of the Day

Name _____

Circle sets of ten.

Write the number of tens and ones.

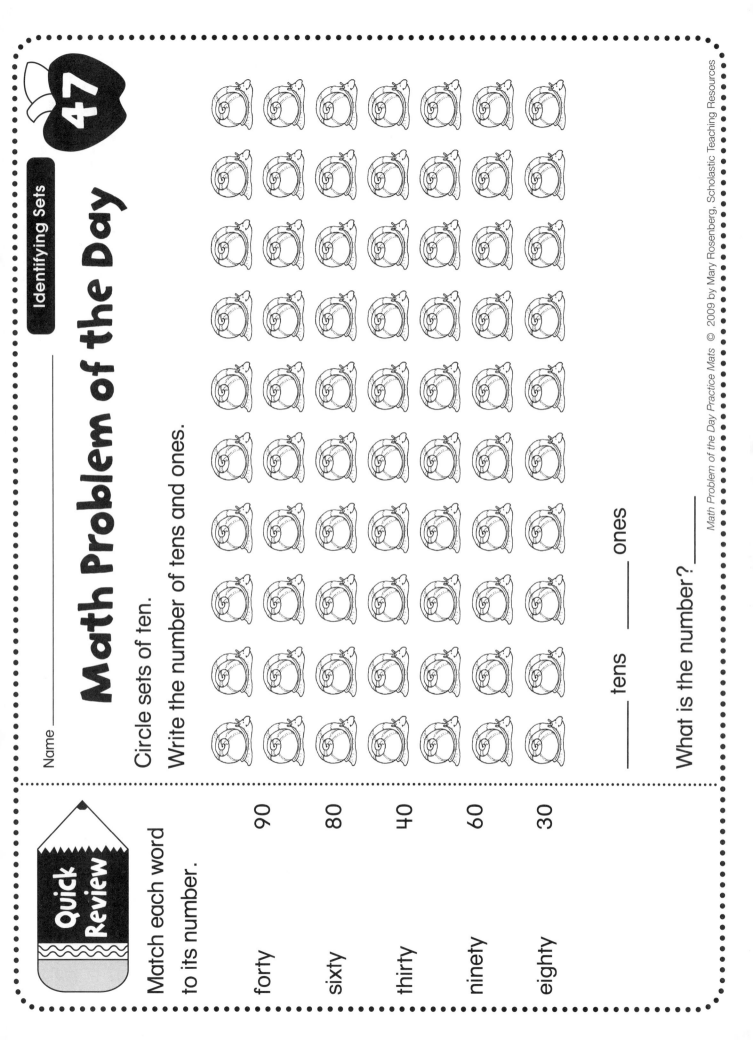

_____ tens _____ ones

What is the number? _____

Quick Review

Match each word to its number.

forty   90

sixty   80

thirty   40

ninety   60

eighty   30

Math Problem of the Day

48

Name _____

Draw raindrops to show the number on the umbrella.

Use sets of tens and ones.

42

Quick Review

Solve each pair of problems.

1. 5 + 1 = _____

1 + 5 = _____

2. 3 + 2 = _____

2 + 3 = _____

3. 6 + 4 = _____

4 + 6 = _____

Math Problem of the Day Practice Mats © 2009 by Mary Rosenberg, Scholastic Teaching Resources

Name _____

Math Problem of the Day

Creating Sets

Draw leaves to show the number on the tree.

Use sets of tens and ones.

59

Quick Review

Solve each pair of problems.

1. 2 + 7 = _____

7 + 2 = _____

2. 8 + 1 = _____

1 + 8 = _____

3. 3 + 4 = _____

4 + 3 = _____

Math Problem of the Day

Name _____

Draw snowballs to show the number on the mitten.
Use sets of tens and ones.

80

Quick Review

Solve each pair
of problems.

1. $6 + 5 =$ _____

   $5 + 6 =$ _____

2. $8 + 9 =$ _____

   $9 + 8 =$ _____

3. $3 + 7 =$ _____

   $7 + 3 =$ _____

Name _____

Identifying Place Value

Math Problem of the Day

Decode the mystery question.

Circle each number in the ones place.

Write the letter on the line that goes with each circled number.

D	S	M	E	O	Y	A	W	N	I
46	17	62	19	30	25	73	11	54	28

H ___ 0 1 ___ 2 3 4 5 ___ 6 3 5 7

8 4 ___ 0 4 9 ___ 1 9 9 ___ K ?

Write the answer: _____

Quick Review

Write the number.

1. _____

2. _____

Name _____

Math Problem of the Day

Decode the mystery question.

Circle each number in the ones place.

Write the letter on the line that goes with each circled number.

O	T	H	Y	M	W	S	A	N	E
31	76	54	13	27	90	48	82	39	85

__ __ __   __ __ __ __   __ __ __ __ __
4 1 0   7 2 9 3   7 1 9 6 4 8

__ __   __ __ __   R ?
9 I   3 5 2

Write the answer: _____

Quick Review

Write the number.

1. _____

2. _____

Name _____

Math Problem of the Day

Decode the mystery question.

Circle each number in the ones place.

Write the letter on the line that goes with each circled number.

M	D	O	Y	R	A	I	N	H	U
80	102	16	91	47	234	59	28	165	73

___ ___   ___ ___ ___ ___
5   6   0   4   8   1
W

___ ___   ___ ___   ___ ___ ___ ___
9   8   4   2   4   1
                              ?

___ ___ ___ ___
5   6   3   7
S

Write the answer: _____

Quick Review

Write the number.

1. _____

2. _____

Math Problem of the Day

Name _____

Decode the mystery question.

Circle each number in the tens place.

Write the letter on the line that goes with each circled number.

A	W	N	I	Y	S	O	E	M	H
29	75	906	191	12	548	361	57	230	84

8 6 7   3 2 0 1   4 5 2 4 6 0 4
‾ ‾ ‾   ‾ ‾ ‾ ‾   ‾ ‾ ‾ ‾ ‾ ‾ ‾

9 0   2   1 5 2   R ?
‾ ‾   ‾   ‾ ‾ ‾

Write the answer: _____

Quick Review

1. 71

How many ones? _____

How many tens? _____

2. 153

How many ones? _____

How many tens? _____

Math Problem of the Day

55

Decode the mystery question.

Circle each number in the tens place.

Write the letter on the line that goes with each circled number.

A	D	E	H	L	O	R	U	W	Y
145	93	319	84	801	52	64	720	276	37

8 5 7   5 0 9

4 6 1   3 5 2   ?

Write the answer: _____

Quick Review

1. 392

How many tens? _____

How many ones? _____

2. 806

How many tens? _____

How many ones? _____

Name _____

Math Problem of the Day

Finish drawing each pattern.

1. △ ○ ○ △ ○

2. ♥ □ ♥ □ ♥

3. ◇ □ ◇ □

4. Use two different shapes to draw an AB pattern.

Quick Review

Sort the shapes.

How many?

triangles _____

squares _____

circles _____

Math Problem of the Day

Name _____

Finish drawing each pattern.

1.

2.

3.

4. Use two different shapes to draw an AAB pattern.

Quick Review

Find the shapes that belong together. Color them the same color.

Name _____

Math Problem of the Day

Finish drawing each pattern.

1.

2.

3.

4. Use two different shapes to draw an ABB pattern.

Quick Review

Sort the numbers.

2 6 1
7 5 3
9 4 8

Odd numbers: _____

Even numbers: _____

Quick Review

Draw an X on the one that doesn't belong.

Name ______________________

Identifying Patterns

59

Math Problem of the Day

Finish drawing each pattern.

1.

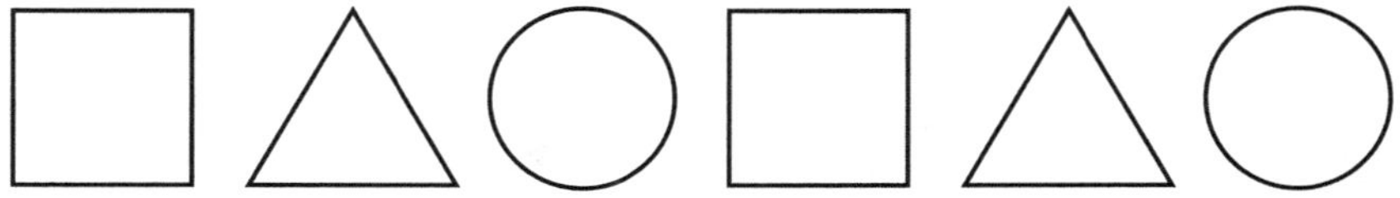

2.

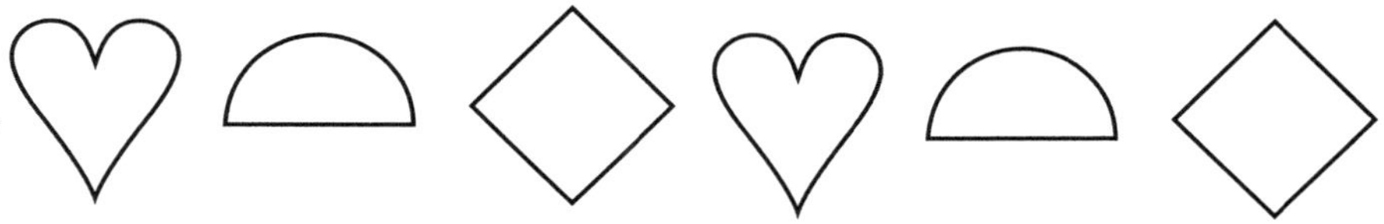

3.

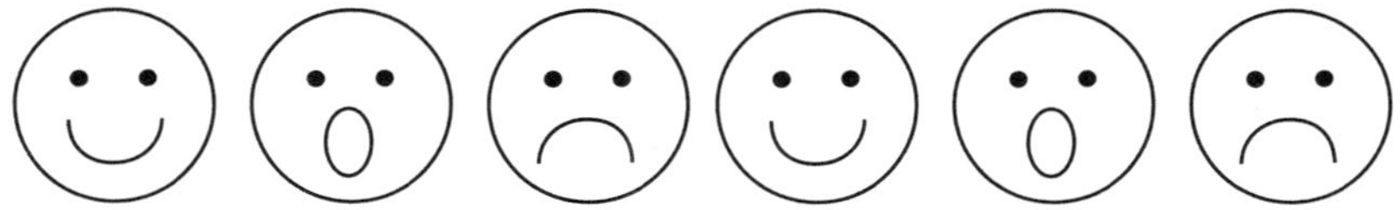

4. Use three different shapes to draw an ABC pattern.

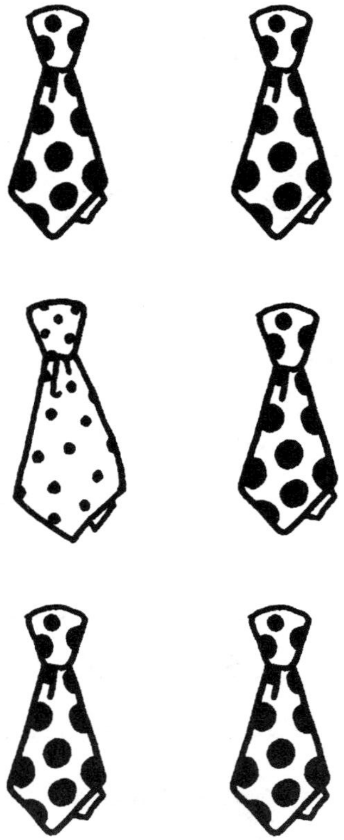

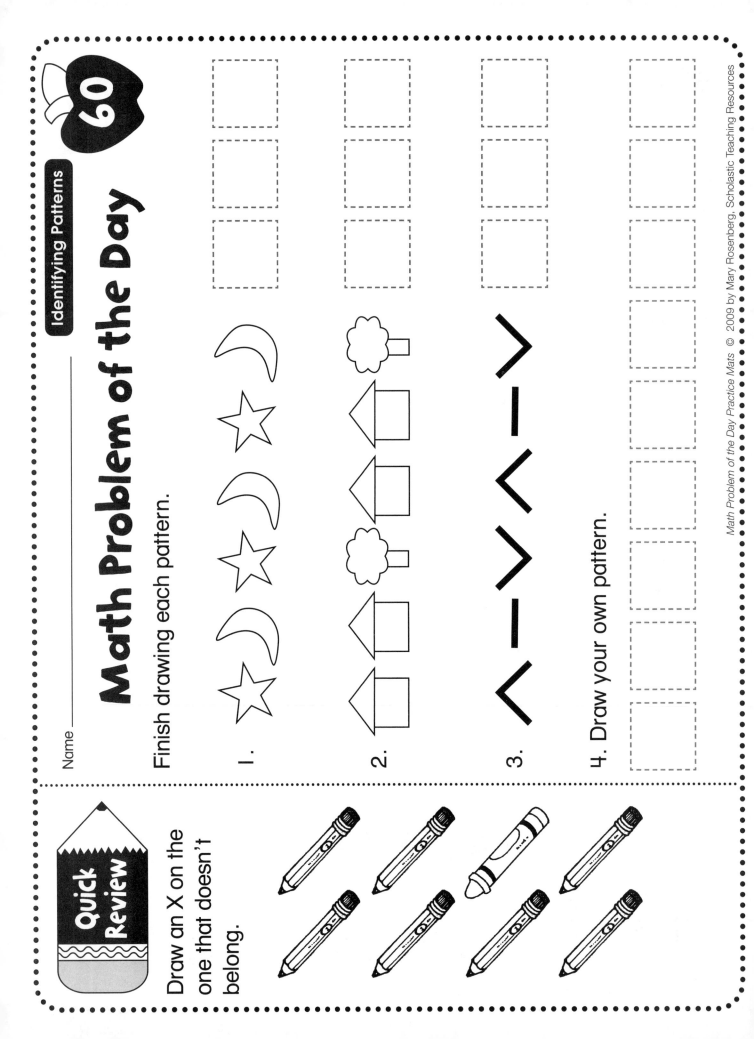

Math Problem of the Day Practice Mats © 2009 by Mary Rosenberg, Scholastic Teaching Resources

Math Problem of the Day

Name _____

Finish drawing each pattern.

1.

2.

3.

4. Draw your own pattern.

Quick Review

Draw an X on the one that doesn't belong.

Math Problem of the Day

Name _____

Finish labeling each pattern.

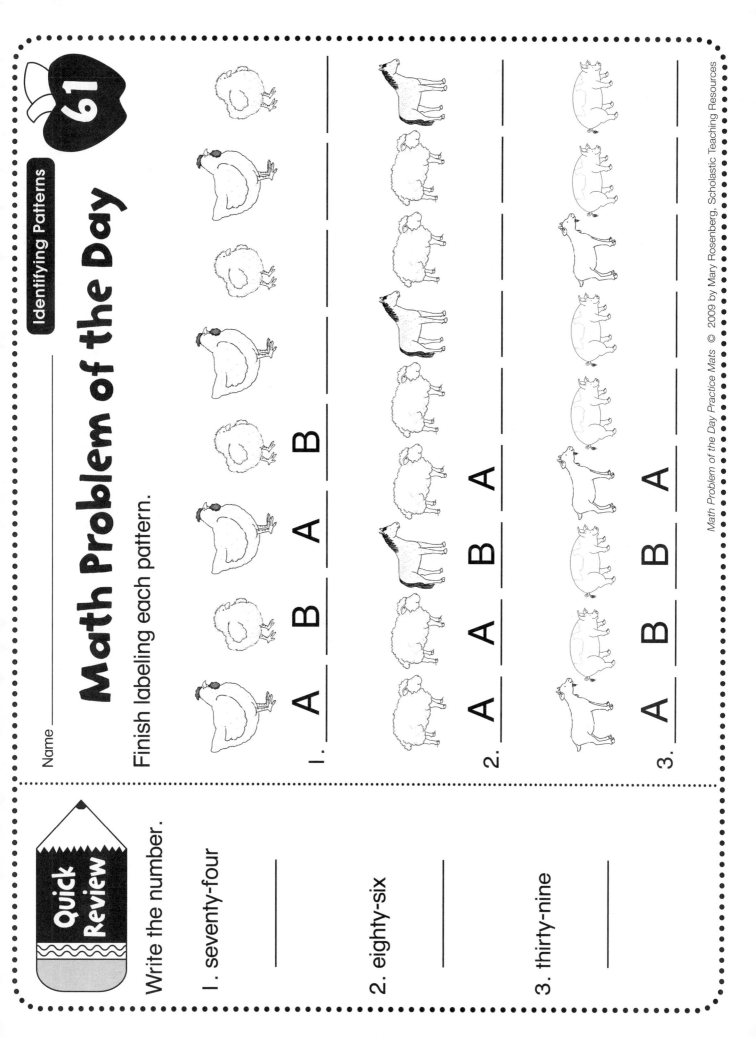

1. A   B   A   B

2. A   A   B   A

3. A   B   B   A

Math Problem of the Day Practice Mats © 2009 by Mary Rosenberg, Scholastic Teaching Resources

Quick Review

Write the number.

1. seventy-four _____

2. eighty-six _____

3. thirty-nine _____

Math Problem of the Day

62

Finish labeling each pattern.

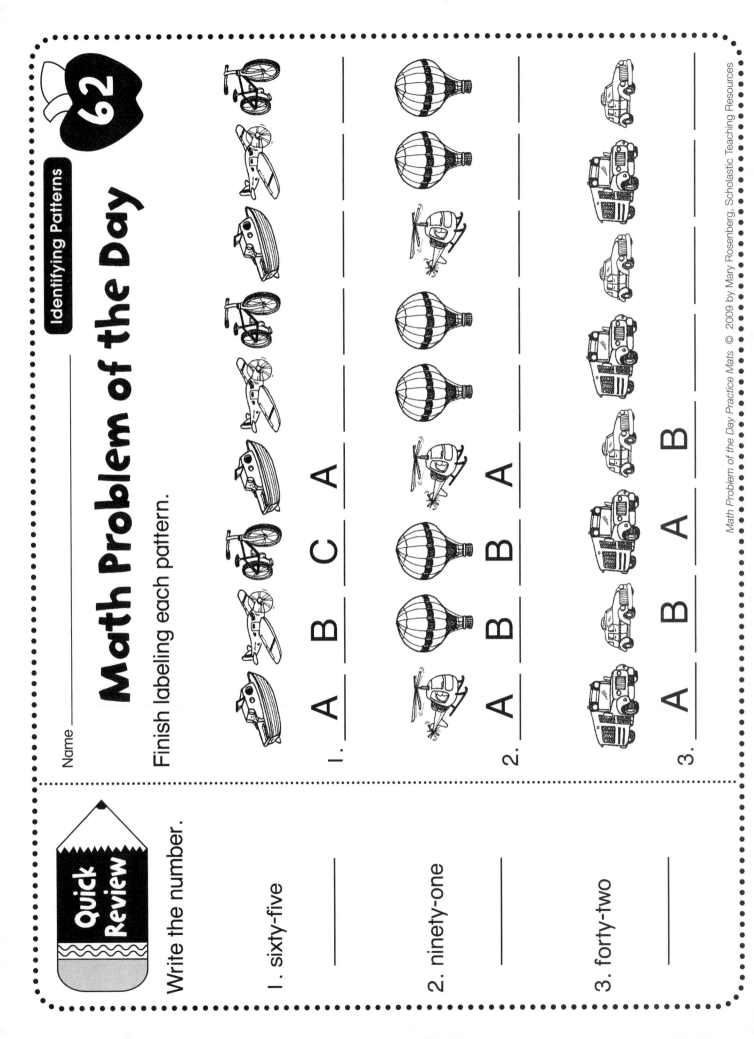

1.   A   B   C   A   A   B   C   A

2.   A   B   B   A   A   B   B   A

3.   A   B   A   B   A   B   A   B

Quick Review

Write the number.

1. sixty-five _____

2. ninety-one _____

3. forty-two _____

Name _____

Math Problem of the Day

Finish labeling each pattern.

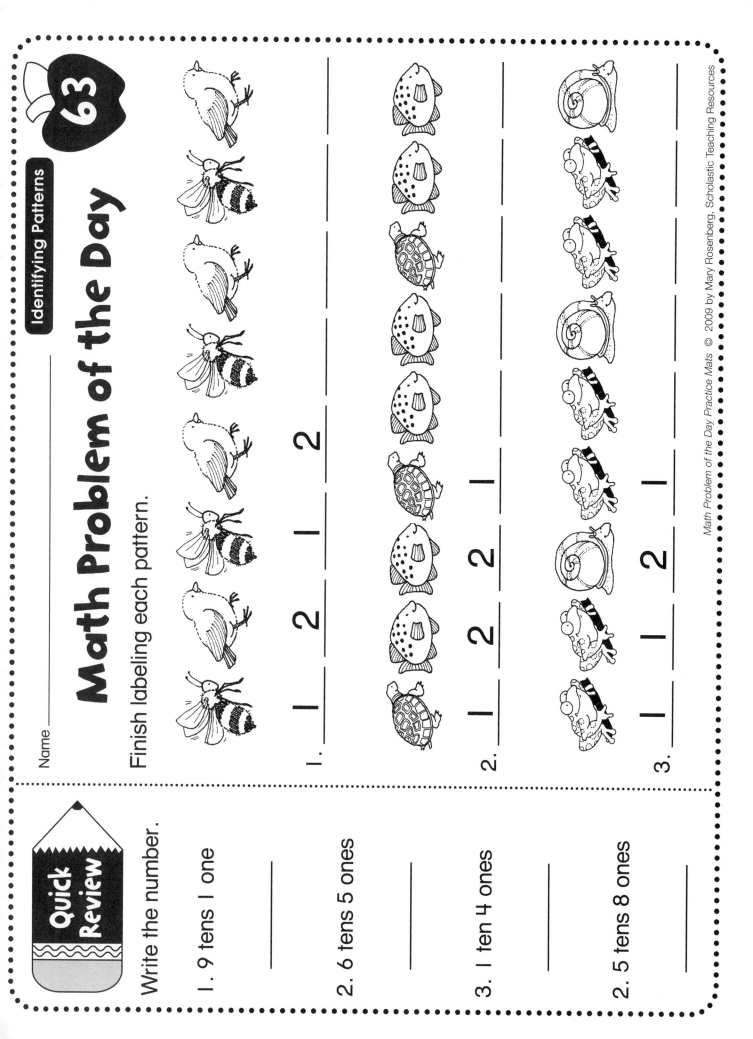

1. ___ 1 ___ 2 ___ 1 ___ 2 ___ 1 ___

2. ___ 1 ___ 2 ___ 2 ___ 1 ___ 2 ___

3. ___ 1 ___ 1 ___ 2 ___ 1 ___ 2 ___ 1 ___

Quick Review

Write the number.

1. 9 tens 1 one _____

2. 6 tens 5 ones _____

3. 1 ten 4 ones _____

2. 5 tens 8 ones _____

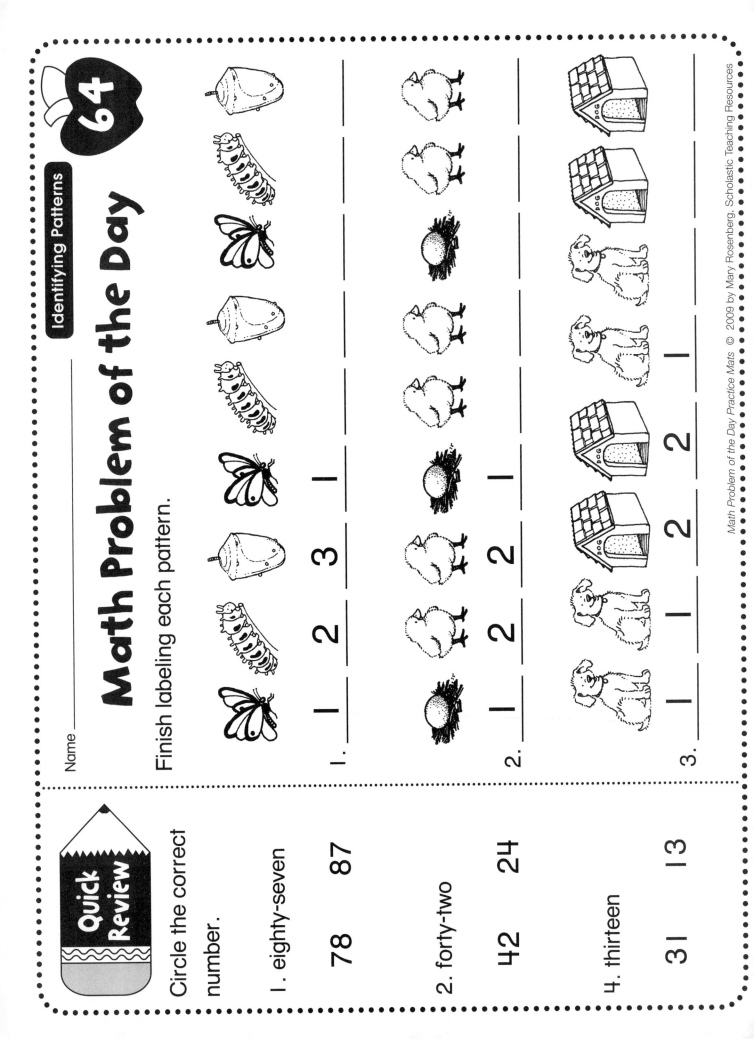

Identifying Patterns

Math Problem of the Day

Finish labeling each pattern.

1. 1 2 3 1 2 3 1

2. 1 2 2 1 2 2 1

3. 1 1 2 2 1 1

Name _____

Quick Review

Circle the correct number.

1. eighty-seven

   78   87

2. forty-two

   42   24

4. thirteen

   31   13

Math Problem of the Day Practice Mats © 2009 by Mary Rosenberg, Scholastic Teaching Resources

Identifying Patterns

Name _____

Math Problem of the Day

Finish each growing pattern.

1. ○   ○○   ○○○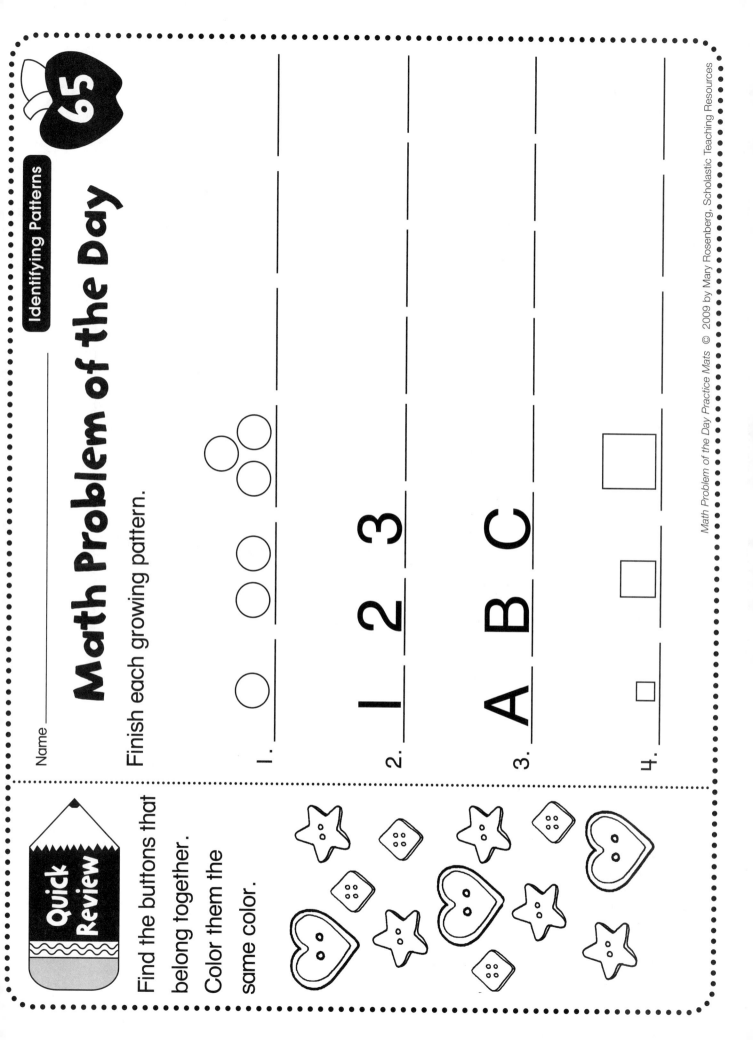

2. 1   2   3 _____ _____

3. A   B   C _____ _____

4. □   □□   □□□

Quick Review

Find the buttons that belong together. Color them the same color.

Name ___

Math Problem of the Day

Look at each pattern. What kind of pattern is it?

Circle the answer.

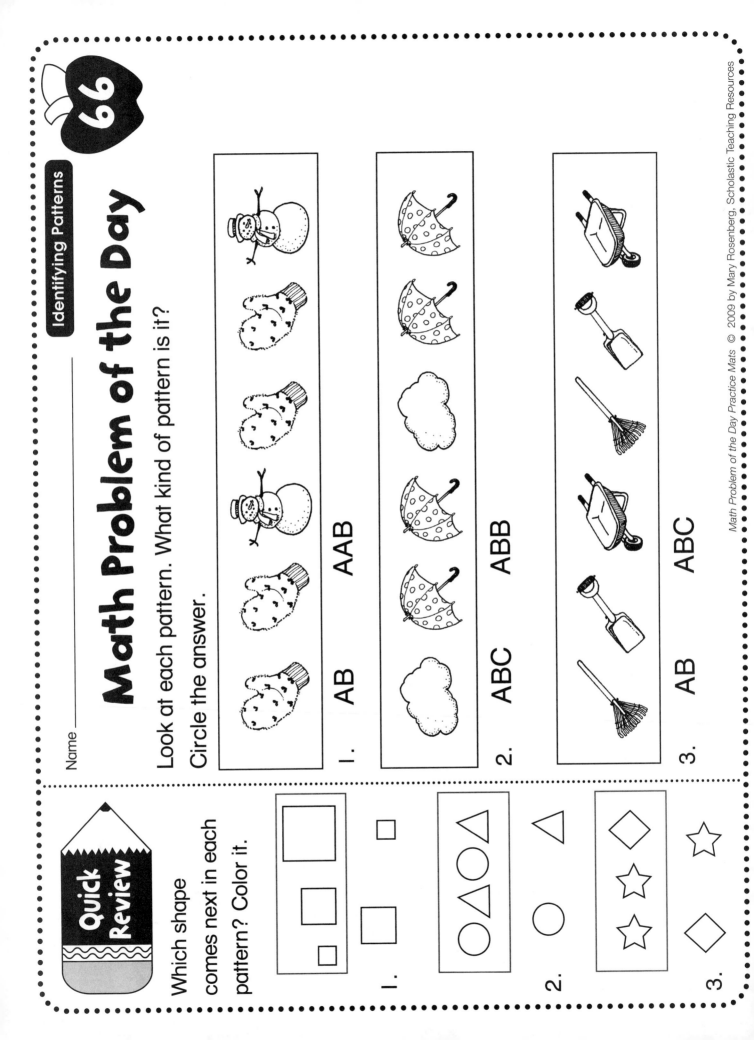

1. AB   AAB

2. ABC   ABB

3. AB   ABC

Quick Review

Which shape comes next in each pattern? Color it.

1.

2.

3.

Identifying Patterns

Math Problem of the Day

Name _____

Make each pattern. Then label the pattern.

Use these shapes: ◯ ☐ △

1. AAB pattern

[ ] [ ] [ ] [ ] [ ] [ ]
___ ___ ___ ___ ___ ___

2. ABC pattern

[ ] [ ] [ ] [ ] [ ] [ ]
___ ___ ___ ___ ___ ___

Quick Review

Write the number that comes next.

1. 2, 4, 6, ___

2. 10, 9, 8, ___

3. 5, 10, 15, ___

4. 0, 1, 2, ___

5. 6, 5, 4, ___

Name _____

Math Problem of the Day

Draw a house. Use these shapes:

- 3 squares   • 2 triangles   • 1 rectangle

Quick Review

1. How many sides?

   square _____

   triangle _____

   rectangle _____

2. Color the small triangles.

Math Problem of the Day Practice Mats © 2009 by Mary Rosenberg, Scholastic Teaching Resources

69

Name _____

Math Problem of the Day

Draw a train. Use these shapes:

• 2 rectangles • 2 squares • 2 triangles • 2 circles

Quick Review

1. Color the square.

2. Color the circle.

3. Color the rectangle.

Math Problem of the Day

Drawing Shapes

70

Draw a space creature. Use these shapes:

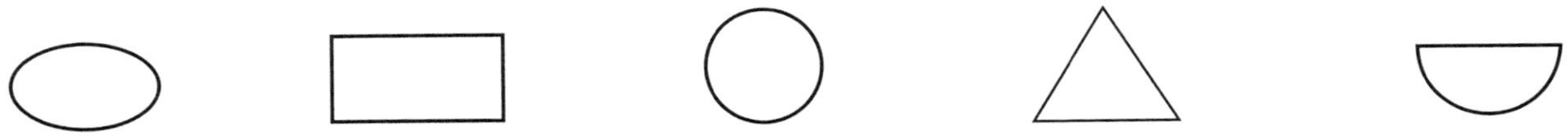

oval   rectangle   circle   triangle   half circle

Quick Review

1. Color the large squares.

2. How many stars?

_____

71

Name _____

Math Problem of the Day

Decorate the frame. Use circles, squares, and triangles. Draw your picture in the frame.

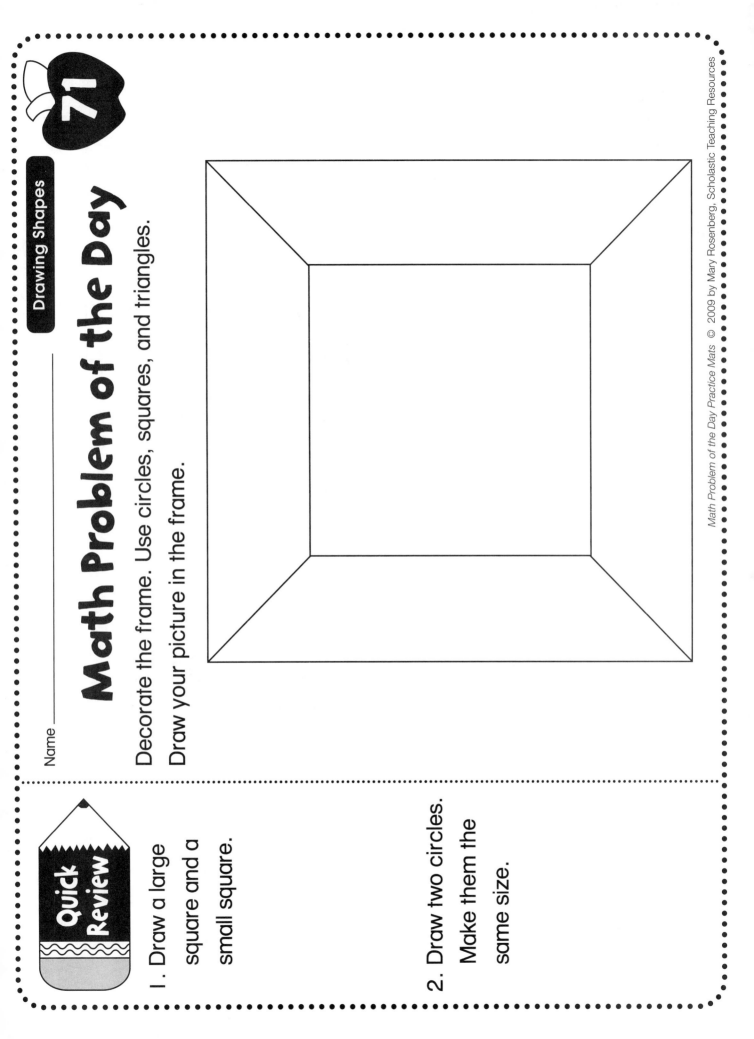

Quick Review

1. Draw a large square and a small square.

2. Draw two circles. Make them the same size.

Name _____

Math Problem of the Day

Use the key to color the shapes.

Then use other colors to finish the picture.

◯ = red   △ = green   ▢ = yellow

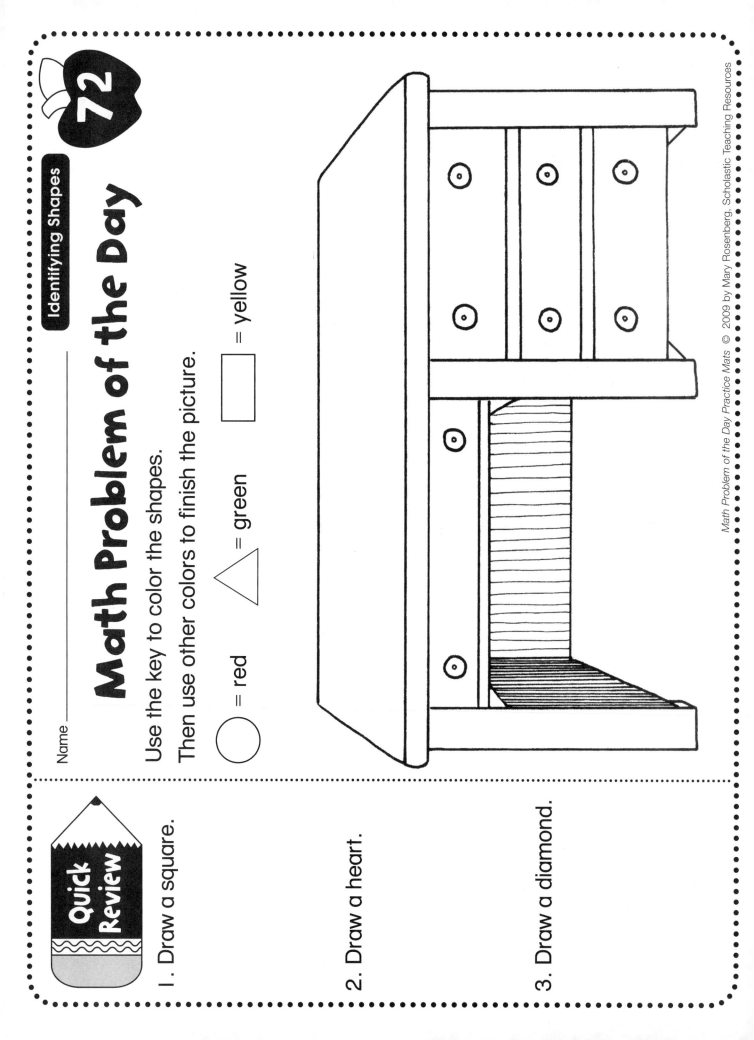

Quick Review

1. Draw a square.

2. Draw a heart.

3. Draw a diamond.

Name _____

Math Problem of the Day

Use the key to color the shapes.

Then use other colors to finish the picture.

- circle = yellow
- rectangle = orange
- triangle = brown
- half circle = black

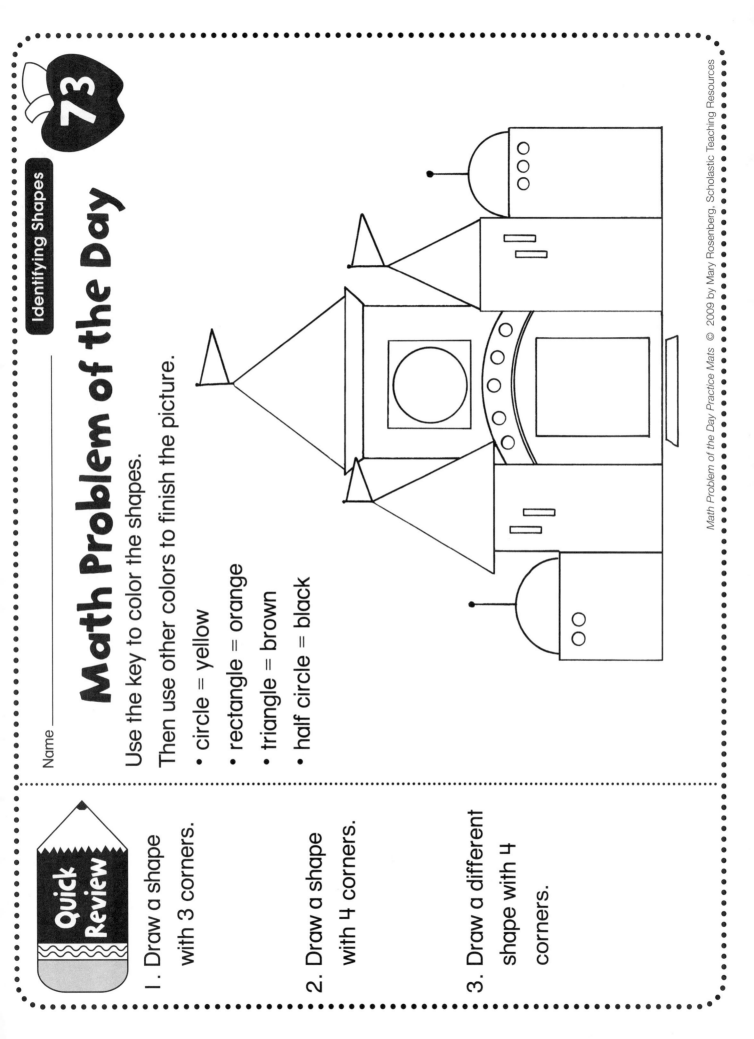

Math Problem of the Day Practice Mats © 2009 by Mary Rosenberg, Scholastic Teaching Resources

Quick Review

1. Draw a shape with 3 corners.

2. Draw a shape with 4 corners.

3. Draw a different shape with 4 corners.

74

Math Problem of the Day

Name _____

Draw a picture of something that has each shape.

circle	square
triangle	rectangle

Quick Review

1. Color the oval.

2. Color the star.

3. Color the heart.

Math Problem of the Day

Name _____

1. Draw a line to make two triangles.

2. Draw two lines to make four equal triangles.

Quick Review

How many corners in each shape?

1. _____ corners

2. _____ corners

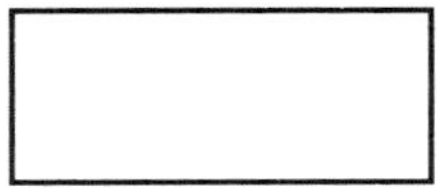

3. _____ corners

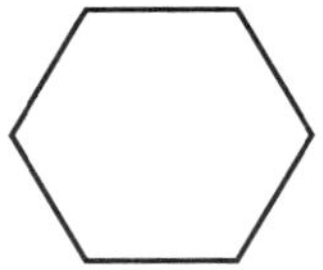

Name _____

Math Problem of the Day

1. Draw a line to make two triangles.

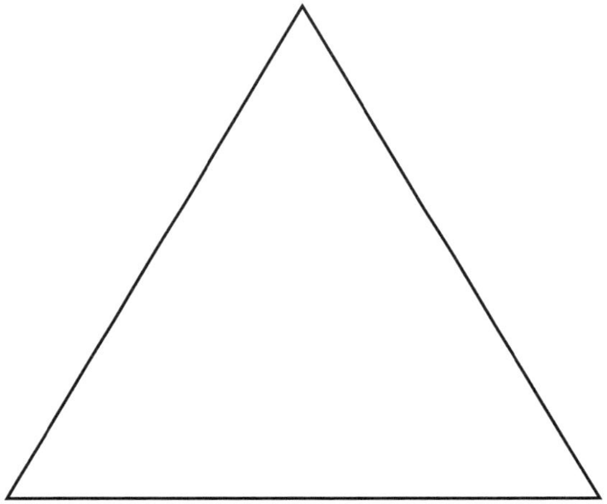

2. Draw lines to make four triangles.

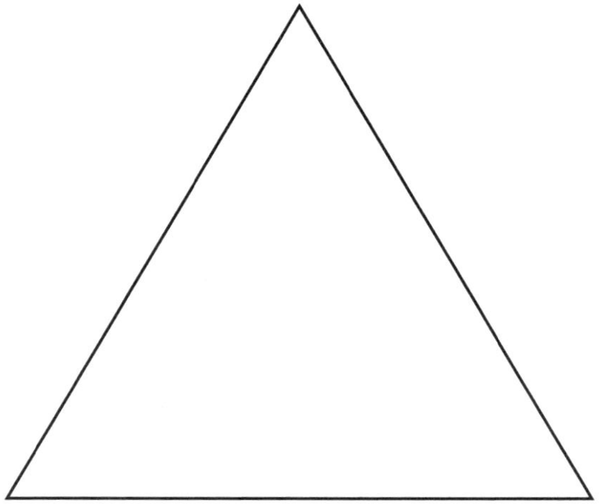

Quick Review

How many corners in each shape?

1. _____ corners

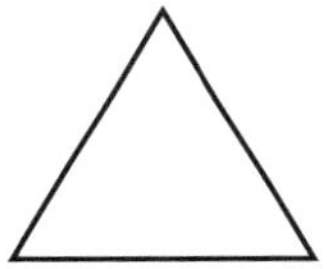

2. _____ corners

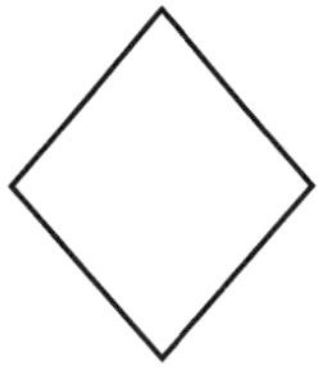

3. _____ corners

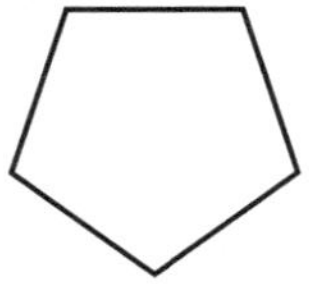

Name _____

Math Problem of the Day

1. Draw a line to make two squares.

2. Draw a line to make two triangles.

Quick Review

How many sides in each shape?

1. _____ sides

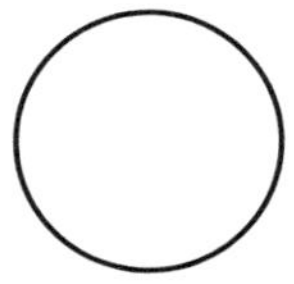

2. _____ sides

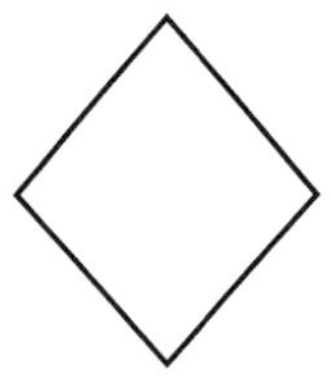

3. _____ sides

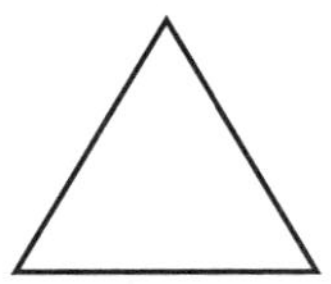

Name _____

Math Problem of the Day

1. Draw a line to make two triangles.

2. Draw a line to make two rectangles.

Quick Review

Circle the name of each shape.

1. cone   cube

2. sphere   cylinder

3. cube   sphere

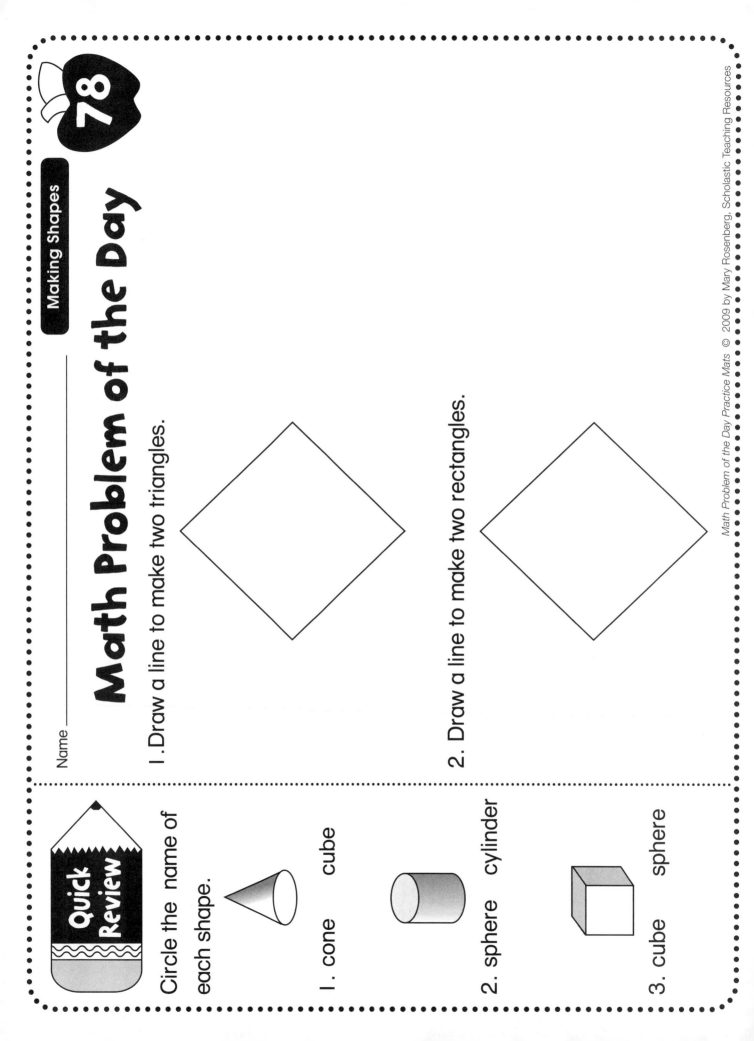

Name _____

Math Problem of the Day

Draw each missing shape.

small	medium	large
	◯	
small	medium	large
		◁
small	medium	large
☐		

Math Problem of the Day Practice Mats © 2009 by Mary Rosenberg, Scholastic Teaching Resources

Quick Review

Match each item to its shape.

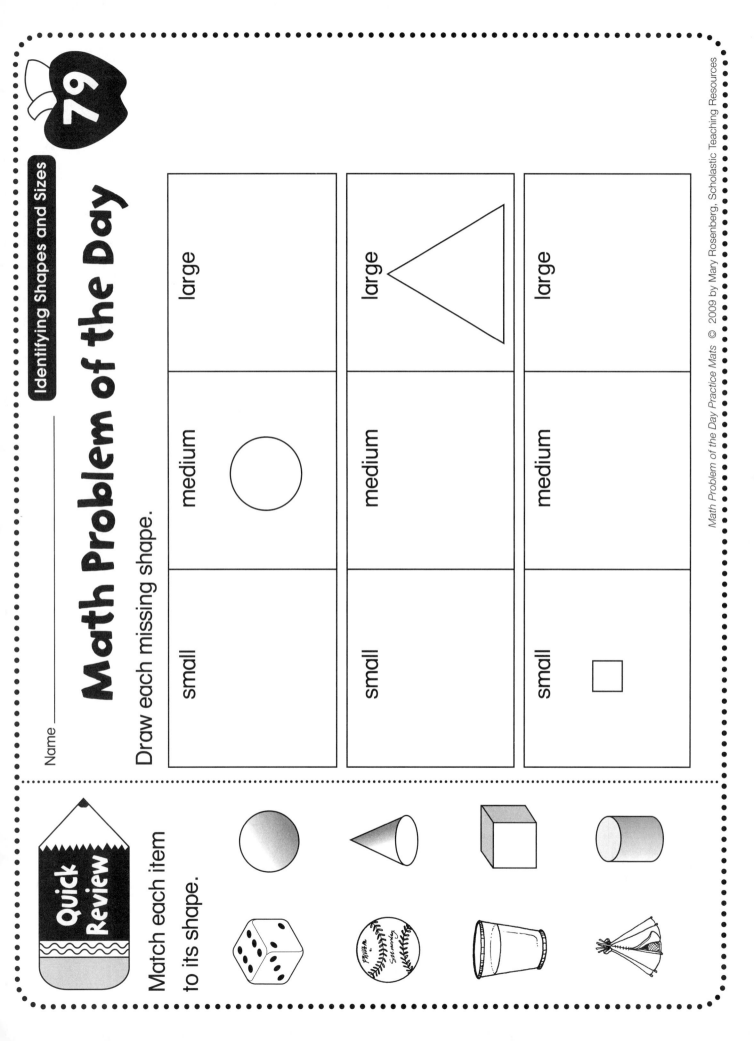

Identifying Symmetry in Shapes

Name _____

Math Problem of the Day

Draw the other half of each shape.

Example:

Quick Review

How many?

triangles _____

squares _____

rectangles _____

Name _____

Math Problem of the Day

Connect the dots to make the same shape on the right.

Answer the questions.

1. What shape did you make? Circle the answer.

   square   triangle   rectangle

2. How many dots did you connect to make the shape? _____ dots

Math Problem of the Day Practice Mats © 2009 by Mary Rosenberg, Scholastic Teaching Resources

Quick Review

Is each half the same size and same shape (symmetrical)?

1. yes   no

2. yes   no

3. yes   no

Name _____

82

Math Problem of the Day

Connect the dots to make a small square on the left. Then make a large square on the right. Answer the questions.

1. How many dots did you connect to make each square?

   small square: _____ dots

   large square: _____ dots

2. Draw a line to divide each square in half.

Quick Review

Is each half the same size and same shape (symmetrical)?

1.   yes   no

2.   yes   no

3.   yes   no

83

Math Problem of the Day

Name _____

Connect the dots to make the same shape on the right.

Answer the questions.

1. What shape did you make? Circle the answer.

   square   triangle   rectangle

2. How many dots did you connect to make the shape? _____ dots

Math Problem of the Day Practice Mats © 2009 by Mary Rosenberg, Scholastic Teaching Resources

Quick Review

Draw a line to divide each item in half.

1.

2.

3.

84

Math Problem of the Day

Name _____

Connect the dots to make a large rectangle on the left.
Then make a small rectangle on the right. Answer the questions.

1. How many dots did you connect to make each rectangle?

    large rectangle: _____ dots

    small rectangle: _____ dots

2. Draw a line to divide each rectangle in half.

Quick Review

Draw a line to divide each item in half symmetrically.

1.

2.

3.

Name _____

Math Problem of the Day

Connect the dots to make the same shape on the right.

Answer the questions.

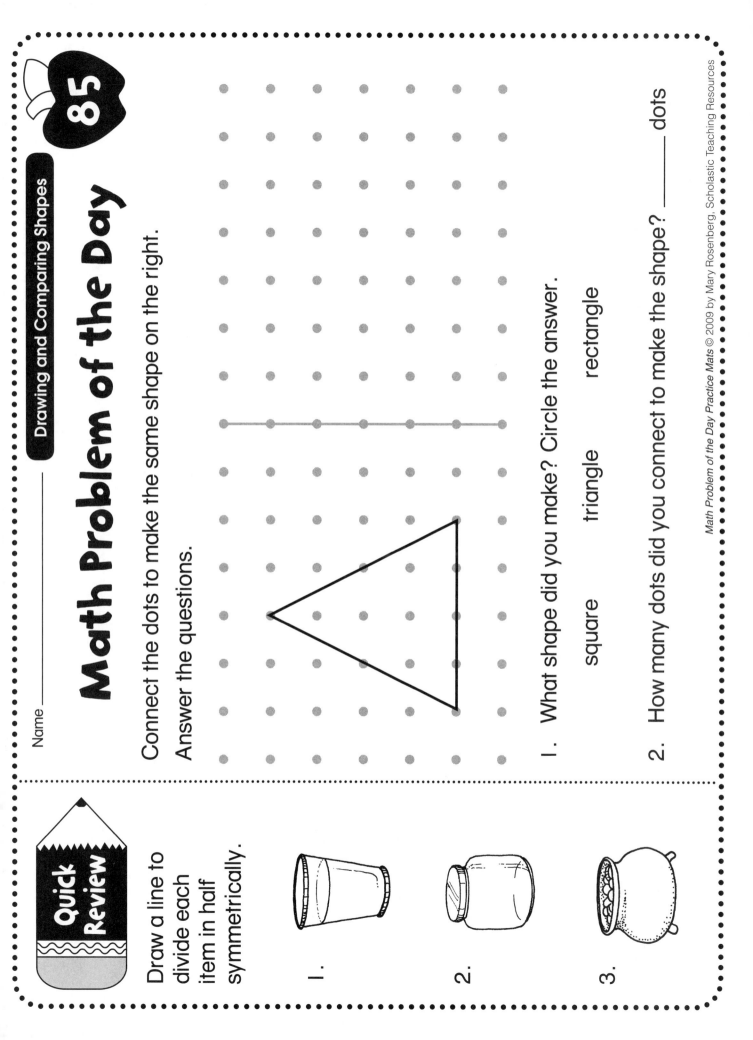

1. What shape did you make? Circle the answer.

   square   triangle   rectangle

2. How many dots did you connect to make the shape? _____ dots

Math Problem of the Day Practice Mats © 2009 by Mary Rosenberg, Scholastic Teaching Resources

Quick Review

Draw a line to divide each item in half symmetrically.

1.

2.

3.

Quick Review

1. How many?

hearts ________

stars ________

diamonds ____

Name ________________

Drawing and Comparing Shapes

86

Math Problem of the Day

Connect the dots to make a rectangle on the left.

Make a triangle on the right.

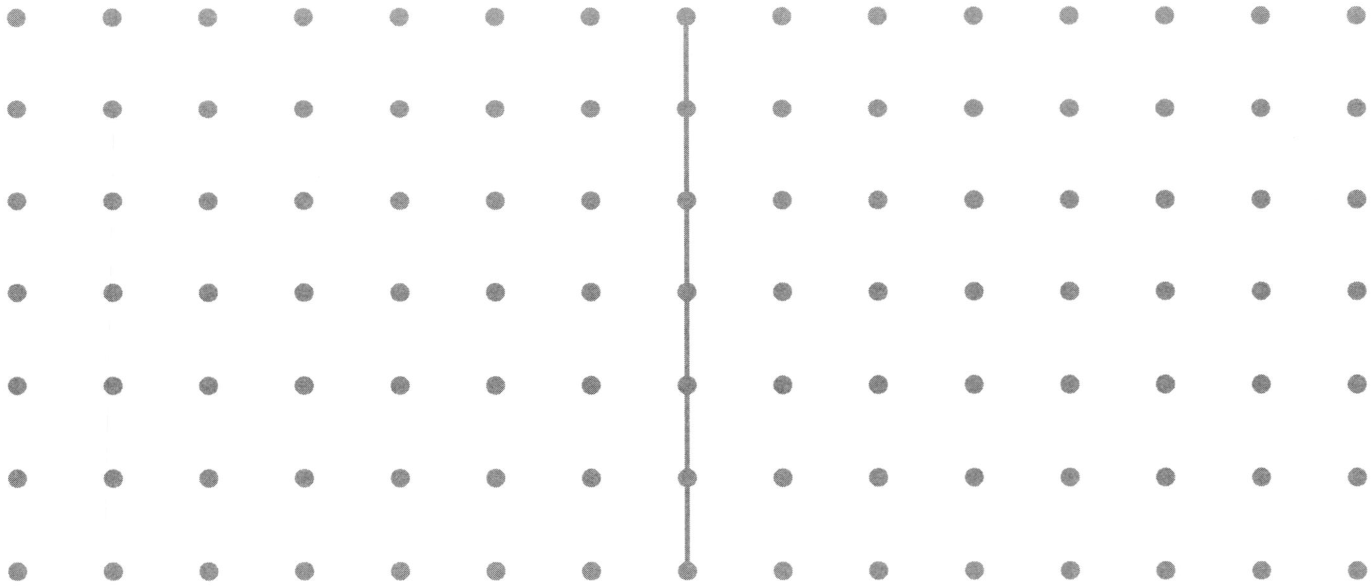

1. How many dots did you connect to make each shape?

rectangle: ______ dots

triangle: ______ dots

2. Draw a line to divide each shape in half.

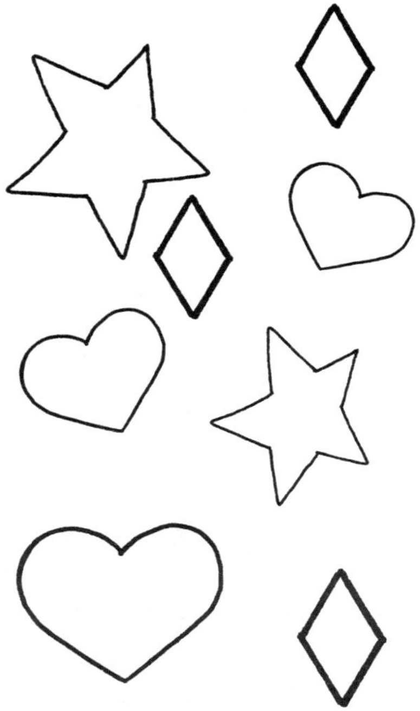

Name _____

Math Problem of the Day

Draw each shape to show its transformation.

1. Turn the shape.

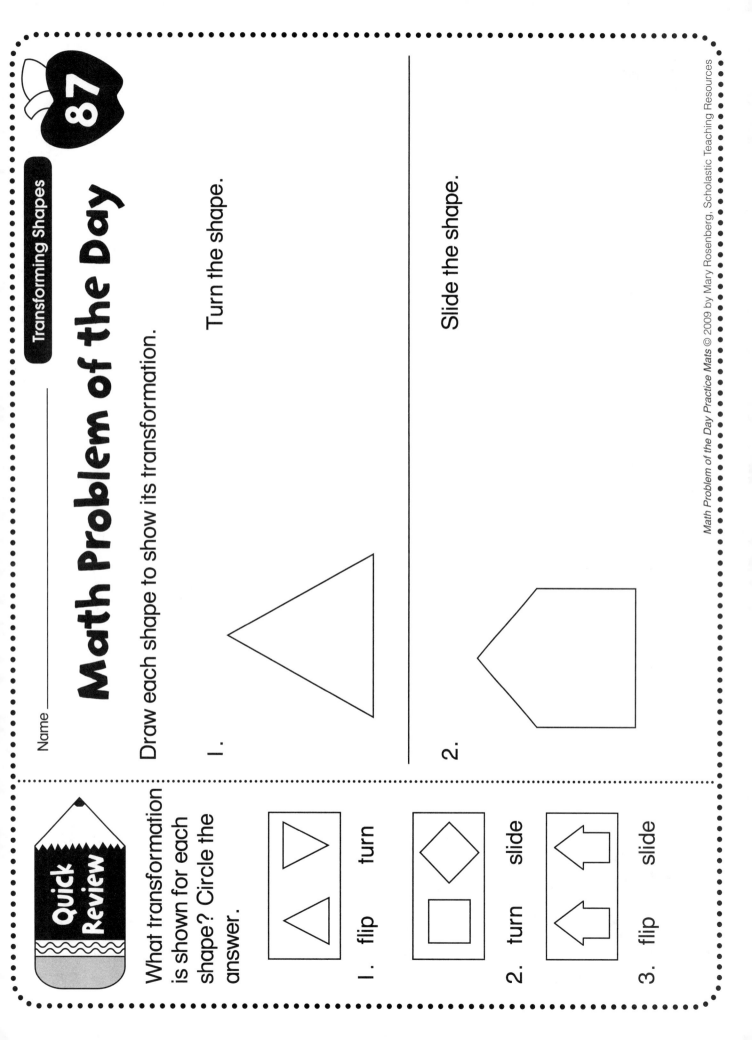

2. Slide the shape.

Quick Review

What transformation is shown for each shape? Circle the answer.

1. flip   turn

2. turn   slide

3. flip   slide

Math Problem of the Day

Name _____

Draw each shape to show its transformation.

1. Turn the shape.

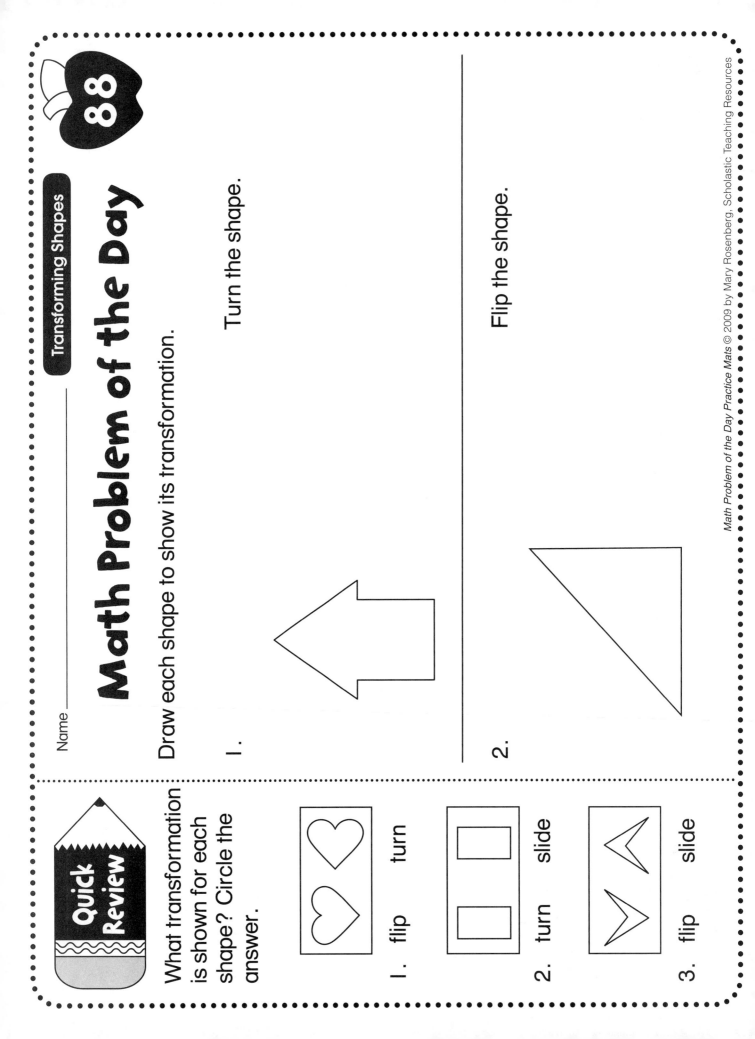

2. Flip the shape.

Quick Review

What transformation is shown for each shape? Circle the answer.

1. flip   turn

2. turn   slide

3. flip   slide

Name _____

Math Problem of the Day

89

Draw the shape to show each transformation.

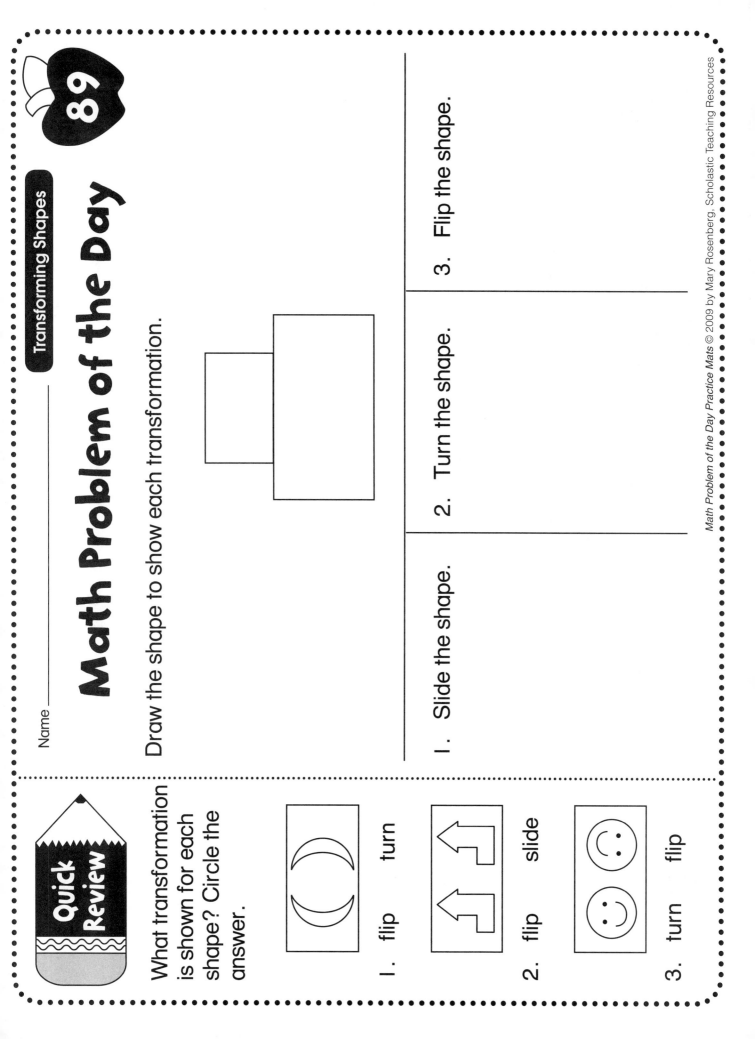

1. Slide the shape.

2. Turn the shape.

3. Flip the shape.

Quick Review

What transformation is shown for each shape? Circle the answer.

1. flip   turn

2. flip   slide

3. turn   flip

Math Problem of the Day Practice Mats © 2009 by Mary Rosenberg, Scholastic Teaching Resources

Math Problem of the Day

Name _____

1. This shape was made with two triangles and one square.
    Draw lines to show how the shapes were put together.

2. Use two triangles and one square to make a different shape.
    Draw the shape.

Quick Review

Draw each transformation.

1. Slide the shape.

2. Turn the shape.

3. Flip the shape.

Name _____

Math Problem of the Day

Answer each question about the classroom. Circle the answer.

chalkboard

window

desk

clock

bookshelf

door

1. What is north of the door?

clock   desk

2. What is west of the bookshelf?

door   window

3. What is east of the window?

desk   chalkboard

4. What is south of the chalkboard?

clock   window

Math Problem of the Day Practice Mats © 2009 by Mary Rosenberg, Scholastic Teaching Resources

Quick Review

1. Start at the dot. Draw a line going north.

●

2. Start at the dot. Draw a line going east.

●

Name _____

Math Problem of the Day

Use the map to answer each question. Circle the answer.

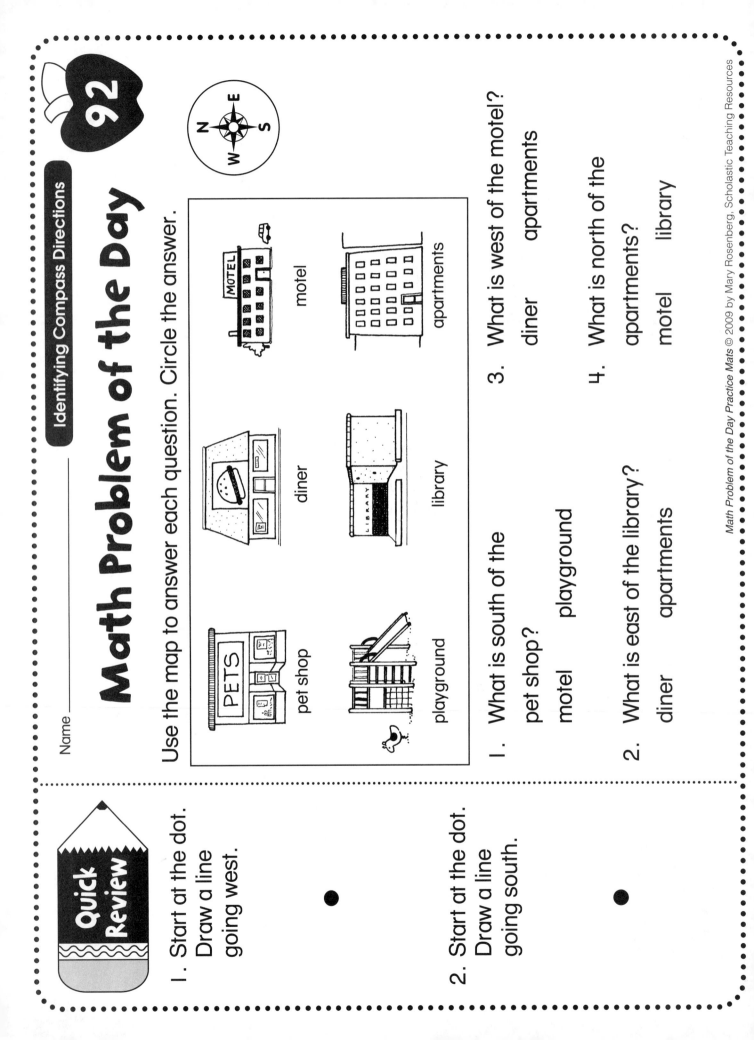

pet shop

diner

motel

playground

library

apartments

1. What is south of the pet shop?

   motel   playground

2. What is east of the library?

   diner   apartments

3. What is west of the motel?

   diner   apartments

4. What is north of the apartments?

   motel   library

Quick Review

1. Start at the dot. Draw a line going west.

   ●

2. Start at the dot. Draw a line going south.

   ●

Name _____

Math Problem of the Day

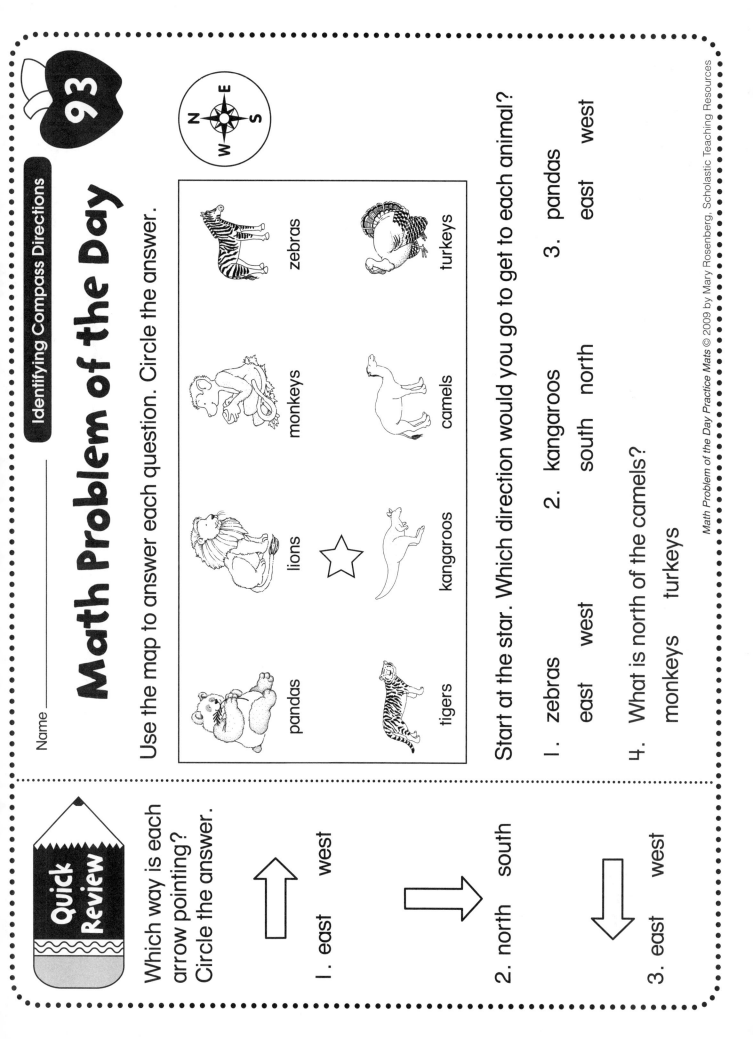

Use the map to answer each question. Circle the answer.

zebras

monkeys

lions

pandas

turkeys

camels

kangaroos

tigers

Start at the star. Which direction would you go to get to each animal?

1. zebras   east   west

2. kangaroos   south   north

3. pandas   east   west

4. What is north of the camels?

   monkeys   turkeys

Math Problem of the Day Practice Mats © 2009 by Mary Rosenberg, Scholastic Teaching Resources

Quick Review

Which way is each arrow pointing? Circle the answer.

1. east   west

2. north   south

3. east   west

Name _____

Math Problem of the Day

Use the map to answer the questions.

sheep   chickens   apple grove

pond   barn   pig

Circle the directions you would go to get to each place.

1. From the barn to
    the pond:

    east   west

2. From the apple grove
    to the pigs:

    north   south

3. From the sheep to the
    apple grove:

    east   west

4. From the chickens to
    the barn:

    north   south

Quick Review

Draw an arrow that points to each direction.

1. North

2. East

3. South

Name _____

Identifying Compass Directions

Math Problem of the Day

Who lives in each house? Write the child's name on the line.

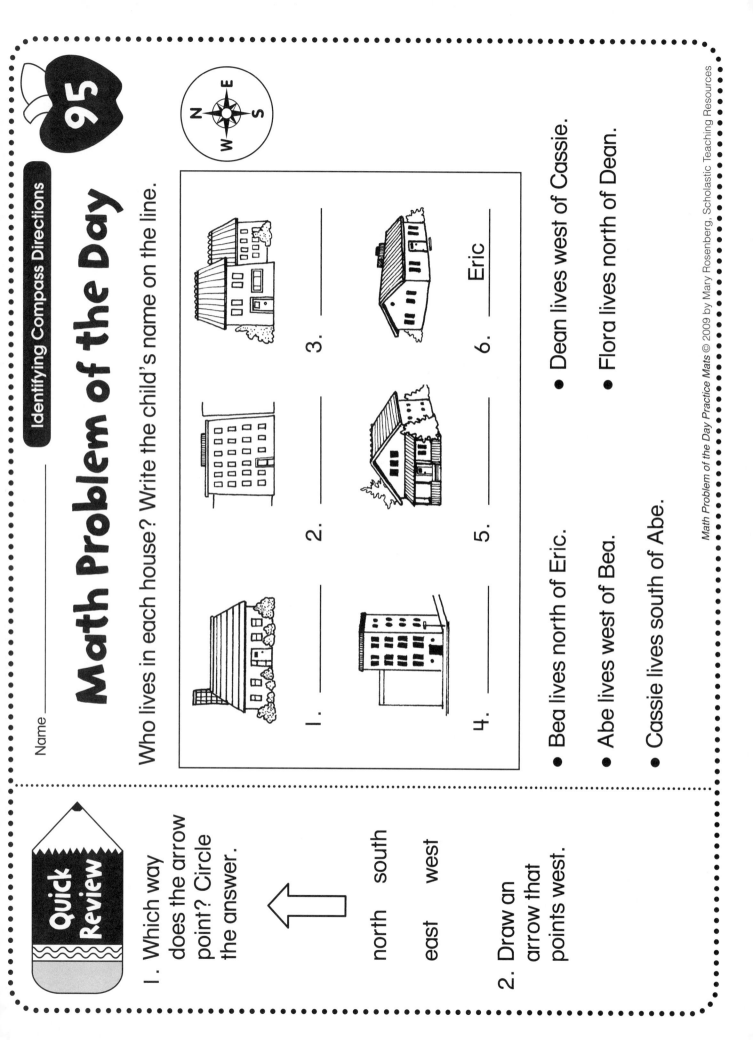

1.

2.

3.

4.

5.

6. _____ Eric

- Bea lives north of Eric.

- Abe lives west of Bea.

- Cassie lives south of Abe.

- Dean lives west of Cassie.

- Flora lives north of Dean.

Quick Review

1. Which way does the arrow point? Circle the answer.

north   south

east   west

2. Draw an arrow that points west.

96

Name _____

Math Problem of the Day

Using Coordinates

Write the name of each item next to its coordinates.

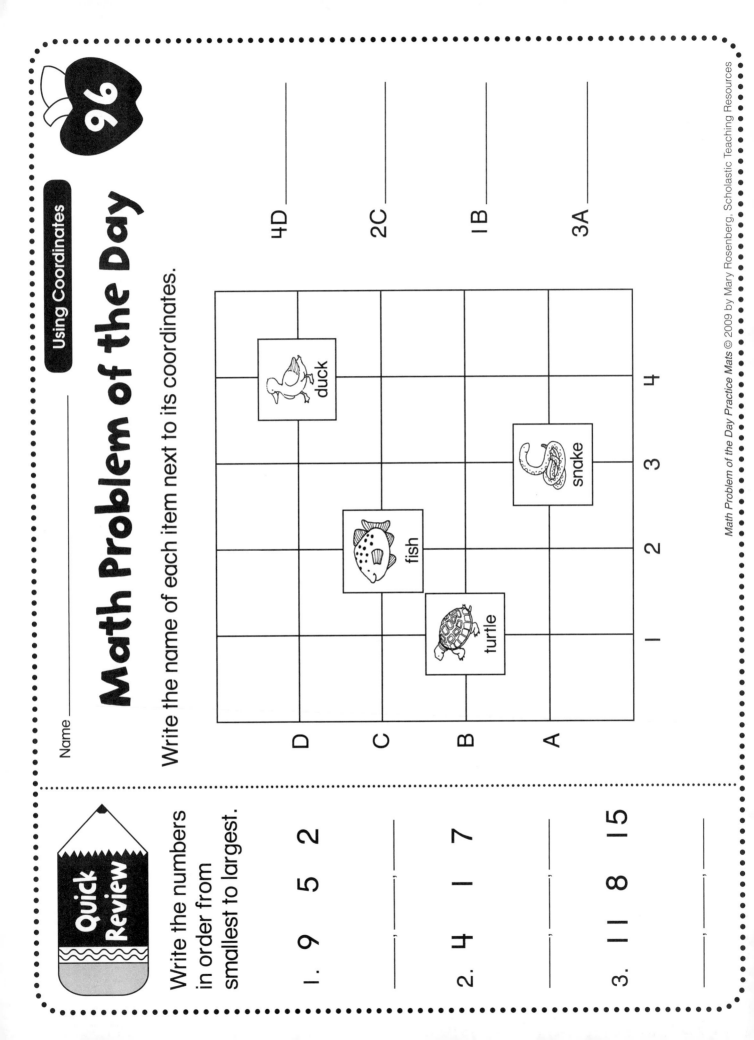

D | | | | duck |
C | | | snake | |
B | | fish | | |
A | turtle | | | |
  | 1 | 2 | 3 | 4 |

4D _____

2C _____

1B _____

3A _____

Quick Review

Write the numbers in order from smallest to largest.

1. 9   5   2

   ___ , ___ , ___

2. 4   1   7

   ___ , ___ , ___

3. 11   8   15

   ___ , ___ , ___

Using Coordinates

Math Problem of the Day

Name _____

Write the name of each item next to its coordinates.

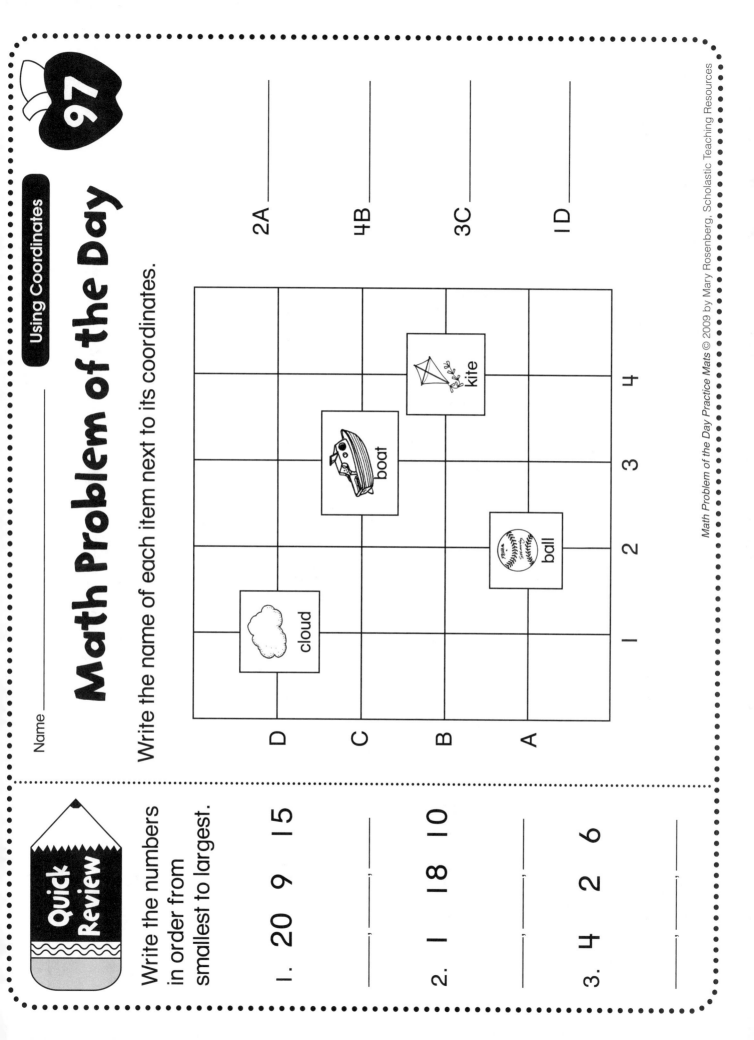

D

cloud

C

boat

B

ball

A

kite

1   2   3   4

2A _____

4B _____

3C _____

1D _____

Math Problem of the Day Practice Mats © 2009 by Mary Rosenberg, Scholastic Teaching Resources

Quick Review

Write the numbers in order from smallest to largest.

1. 20   9   15

___ ___ ___

2. 1   18   10

___ ___ ___

3. 4   2   6

___ ___ ___

Name _____

Math Problem of the Day

Using Coordinates

Write the name of each item next to its coordinates.

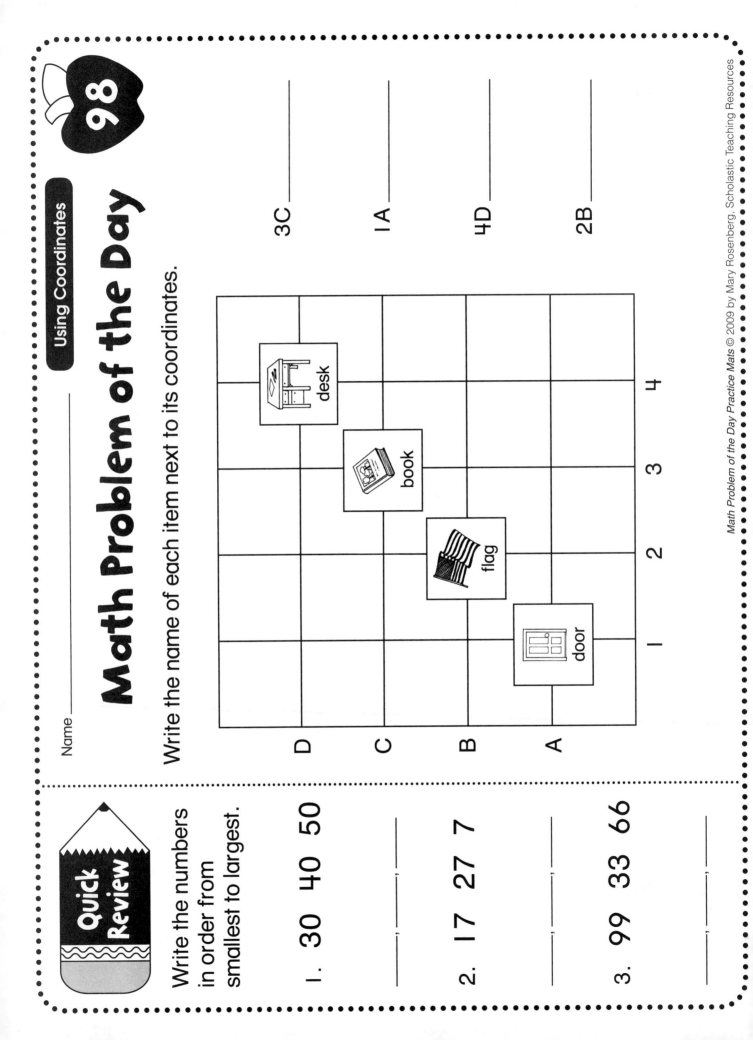

	1	2	3	4
D				desk
C			book	
B		flag		
A	door			

3C _____

1A _____

4D _____

2B _____

Quick Review

Write the numbers in order from smallest to largest.

1. 30 40 50

_____

2. 17 27 7

_____

3. 99 33 66

_____

Name _____

Using Coordinates

Math Problem of the Day

Write the coordinates for each item.

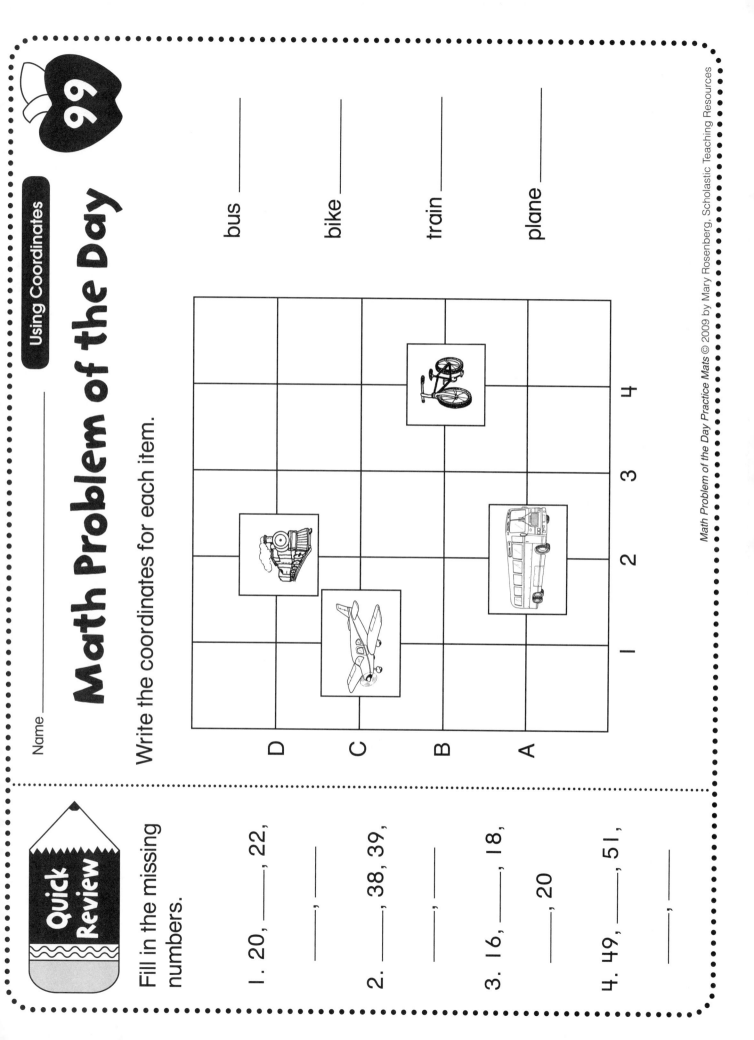

D | | | | |
C | | | | |
B | | | | |
A | | | | |
   1   2   3   4

bus _____

bike _____

train _____

plane _____

Quick Review

Fill in the missing numbers.

1. 20, _____, 22, _____

   _____, _____

2. _____, 38, 39, _____

   _____

3. 16, _____, 18, _____

   _____, 20

4. 49, _____, 51, _____

   _____, _____

Name _____

Using Coordinates

Math Problem of the Day

Write the coordinates for each item.

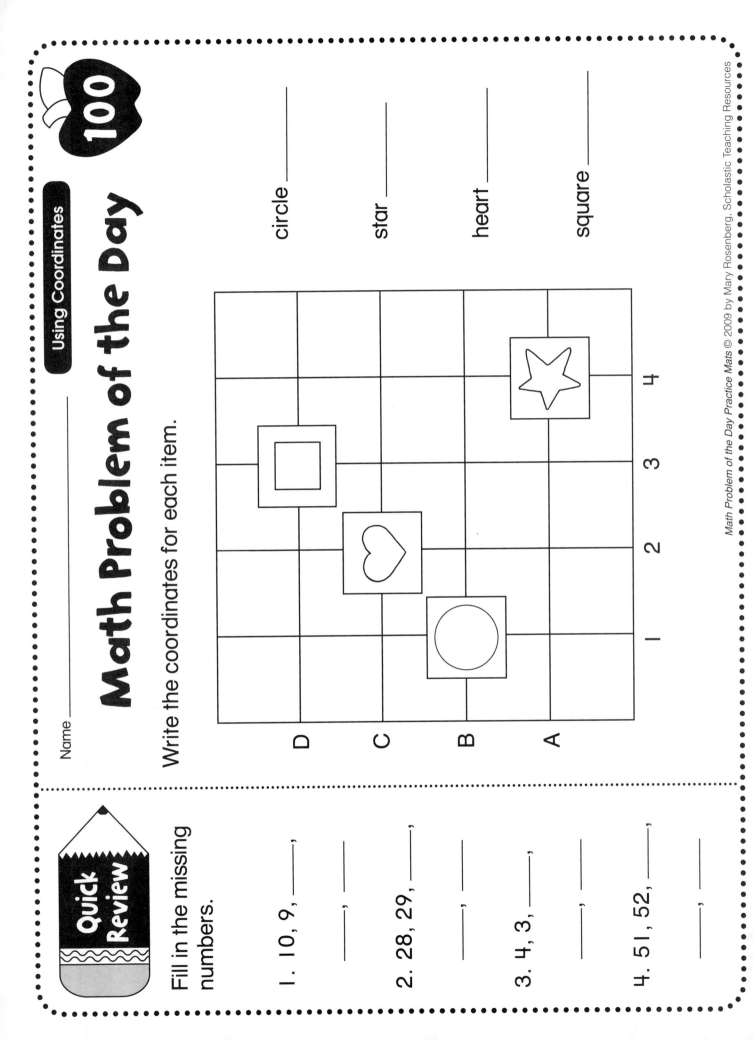

D			☐	
C		♡		
B	◯			
A				☆
	1	2	3	4

circle _____

star _____

heart _____

square _____

Quick Review

Fill in the missing numbers.

1. 10, 9, ____, ____

2. 28, 29, ____, ____

3. 4, 3, ____, ____

4. 51, 52, ____, ____

Math Problem of the Day

Solve each word problem. Draw a picture to show how you solved it.

1. Amy had 6 pieces of candy. Her mother gave her 4 more pieces.

How many pieces of candy does Amy have?

_____ pieces of candy

2. Danny had 5 cookies. His sister game him 3 more cookies.

How many cookies does Danny have?

_____ cookies

Quick Review

Count by 2s.
Write the numbers.

1. _____

2. _____, _____

3. _____, _____, _____

Math Problem of the Day

Name _____

Solve each word problem. Draw a picture to show how you solved it.

1. Neal had 4 baseballs. He caught 2 baseballs at the game. How many baseballs does Neal have?

_____ baseballs

2. Mia had 3 dolls. She bought 4 more dolls at the flea market. How many dolls does Mia have?

_____ dolls

Quick Review

Count by 5s.
Write the numbers.

1. _____

2. _____ _____

3. _____ _____ _____

Solving Word Problems

Math Problem of the Day

Name _____

Solve each word problem. Draw a picture to show how you solved it.

1. Ben planted 3 flowers in a flower pot. He planted 5 flowers in another flower pot. How many flowers does Ben have?

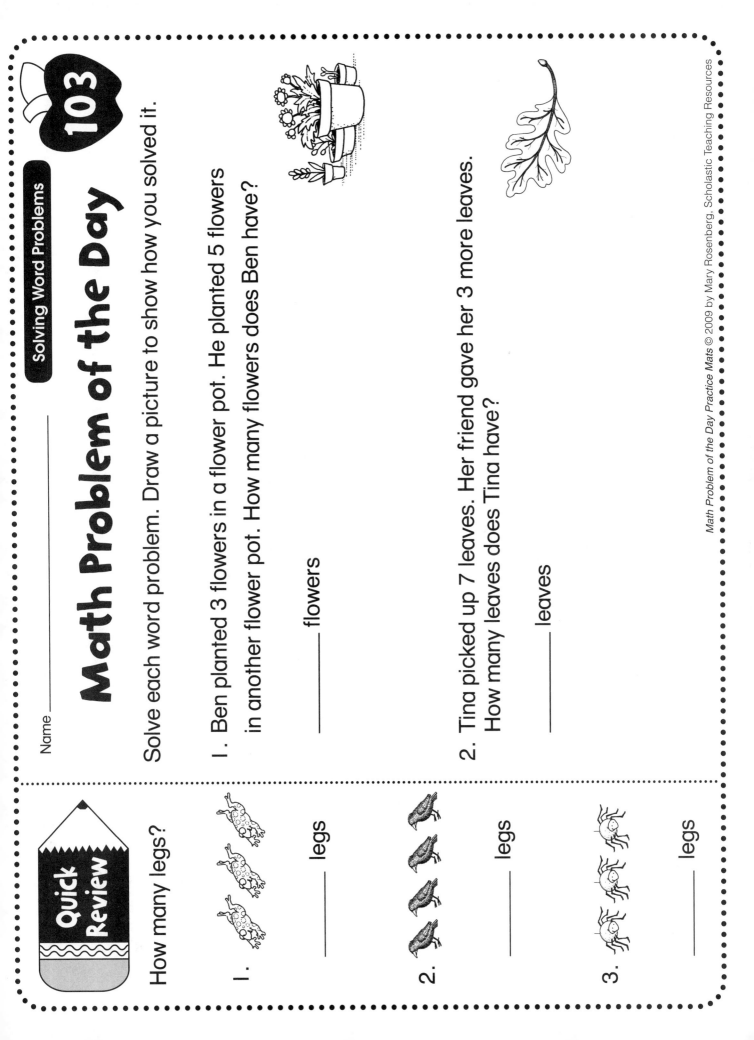

_____ flowers

2. Tina picked up 7 leaves. Her friend gave her 3 more leaves. How many leaves does Tina have?

_____ leaves

Math Problem of the Day Practice Mats © 2009 by Mary Rosenberg, Scholastic Teaching Resources

Quick Review

How many legs?

1.

_____ legs

2.

_____ legs

3.

_____ legs

Name _____

Math Problem of the Day

Solving Word Problems

Solve each word problem. Draw a picture to show how you solved it.

1. 10 ants crawled up a fence. 6 more ants joined them.
How many ants are on the fence?

_____ ants

2. 7 snakes hid under a bush. 8 more snakes joined them.
How many snakes are under the bush?

_____ snakes

Quick Review

1. How many tails?

_____ tails

2. How many ears?

_____ ears

3. How many arms?

_____ arms

Math Problem of the Day

Name _____

Solve each word problem. Draw a picture to show how you solved it.

1. Tracy had 10 crayons. She lost 4 crayons on her way to school.

How many crayons does Tracy have left?

_____ crayons

2. Rob had 8 rulers. He gave 6 rulers to his friends.
How many rulers does Rob have left?

_____ rulers

Quick Review

Count backwards.
Fill in the missing
numbers.

1. 5, 4, ____, ____

2. 10, ____, ____

3. 14, ____, ____

4. 7, ____, ____

Math Problem of the Day Practice Mats © 2009 by Mary Rosenberg, Scholastic Teaching Resources

Math Problem of the Day

Name _____

Solve each word problem. Draw a picture to show how you solved it.

1. Grandpa had 12 slices of pie. He gave 9 slices to his grandchildren. How many slices of pie does Grandpa have left?

_____ slices

2. Mom popped 17 bags of popcorn. She gave 11 bags to the children in class. How many bags of popcorn does Mom have left?

_____ bags

Quick Review

Use Xs to show how to solve each problem.

1. $10 - 3 =$ _____

2. $8 - 5 =$ _____

2. $13 - 9 =$ _____

Math Problem of the Day Practice Mats © 2009 by Mary Rosenberg, Scholastic Teaching Resources

Name _____

Math Problem of the Day

Solve each word problem. Draw a picture to show how you solved it.

1. Pudgy buried 18 bones last week. He dug up 6 bones today. How many bones are still buried?

_____ bones

2. Squirrel had 13 acorns in her nest. She moved 7 acorns to a hole in the ground. How many acorns are left in Squirrel's nest?

_____ acorns

Quick Review

Use each set of numbers to make two subtraction problems.

1. 3, 5, 8

___ − ___ = ___

___ − ___ = ___

2. 2, 6, 8

___ − ___ = ___

___ − ___ = ___

Math Problem of the Day

Name _____

Solve each word problem. Draw a picture to show how you solved it.

1. Joe had 9 cups. He used 7 cups to set the table. How many cups does he have left?

_____ cups

2. Bea bought 11 cans of fruit drink. She gave away 5 cans at her sister's party. How many cans of fruit drink does Bea have left?

_____ cans

Quick Review

Use each set of numbers to make two subtraction problems.

1. 4, 5, 9

_____ − _____ = _____

_____ − _____ = _____

2. 3, 7, 10

_____ − _____ = _____

_____ − _____ = _____

Math Problem of the Day

Name _____

Solve each word problem.

1. The dog weighs more than the cat. The cat weighs more than the bird. Circle the animal that weighs the most.

bird   cat   dog

2. Bob is older than Claire. Tim is older than Bob. Circle the oldest person.

Bob   Claire   Tim

Quick Review

1. Color the shape with the most sides.

2. Color the smallest shape.

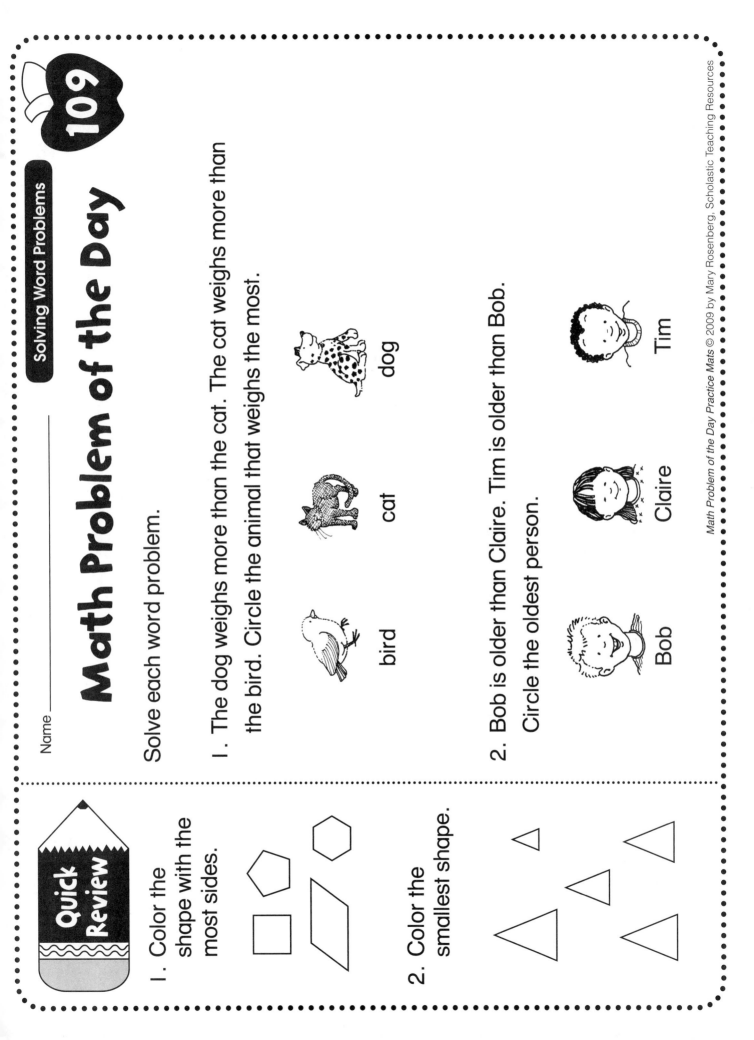

Math Problem of the Day Practice Mats © 2009 by Mary Rosenberg, Scholastic Teaching Resources

Solving Word Problems

Math Problem of the Day

Name _____

Solve each word problem.

1. Bryan is taller than Marie. Pam is taller than Bryan. Circle the tallest person.

Bryan   Marie   Pam

2. The pencil weighs more than the paper. The pencil weighs less than the glue stick. Circle the one that weighs the least.

paper   glue stick   pencil

Quick Review

1. Color the heaviest one.

2. Color the shortest one.

Name _____

Solving Word Problems

Math Problem of the Day

Solve each word problem.

1. The jug holds more than the cup. The tub holds more than the jug. Circle the one that holds the most.

jug   tub   cup

2. The penny is bigger than the dime. The penny is smaller than the quarter. Circle the biggest coin.

dime   penny   quarter

Quick Review

1. Color the longest one.

2. Color the one with the most legs.

Math Problem of the Day

Name _____

Solve the word problem. Draw a picture to help you.

I have a bag of cookies.

I share the cookies with two friends.

My friends each share the cookies with two friends.

How many people have cookies?

_____ people

Quick Review

Solve each problem.

1. 5 + 5 = _____

2. 9 + 1 = _____

3. 3 + 3 = _____

4. 4 + 5 = _____

5. 3 + 4 = _____

6. 5 + 6 = _____

Name _____

Math Problem of the Day

Solve the word problem. Draw a picture to help you.

Genie has five fingers.

She puts two rings on each finger.

How many rings does Genie have in all?

_____ rings

Quick Review

Solve each problem.

1. $3 + 6 =$ _____

2. $3 + 4 =$ _____

3. $6 + 6 =$ _____

4. $4 + 4 =$ _____

5. $6 + 7 =$ _____

6. $9 + 9 =$ _____

Math Problem of the Day Practice Mats © 2009 by Mary Rosenberg, Scholastic Teaching Resources

Math Problem of the Day Practice Mats © 2009 by Mary Rosenberg, Scholastic Teaching Resources

Solving Word Problems

Math Problem of the Day

Solve the word problem. Draw a picture to help you.

Rose has 16 balloons.

She gives 8 balloons to her friend.

Then she gives 4 balloons to her sister.

How many balloons does Rose have left?

_____ balloons

Quick Review

Solve each problem.

1. $1 + 2 =$ _____

2. $7 + 8 =$ _____

3. $2 + 3 =$ _____

4. $8 + 8 =$ _____

5. $7 + 6 =$ _____

6. $3 + 8 =$ _____

Name _____

Math Problem of the Day

Solving Word Problems

Solve the word problem. Draw a picture to help you.

Wade has 20 cards.

He gives 10 to Noah.

Then he gives 6 cards to Patsy.

How many cards does Wade have left?

_____ cards

Quick Review

Write another addition problem with the same numbers.

1. 8 + 5 = 13

_____ + _____ = _____

2. 7 + 5 = 12

_____ + _____ = _____

3. 6 + 9 = 15

_____ + _____ = _____

Name _____

Math Problem of the Day

How many leaves long is each item? Write the answer.

1.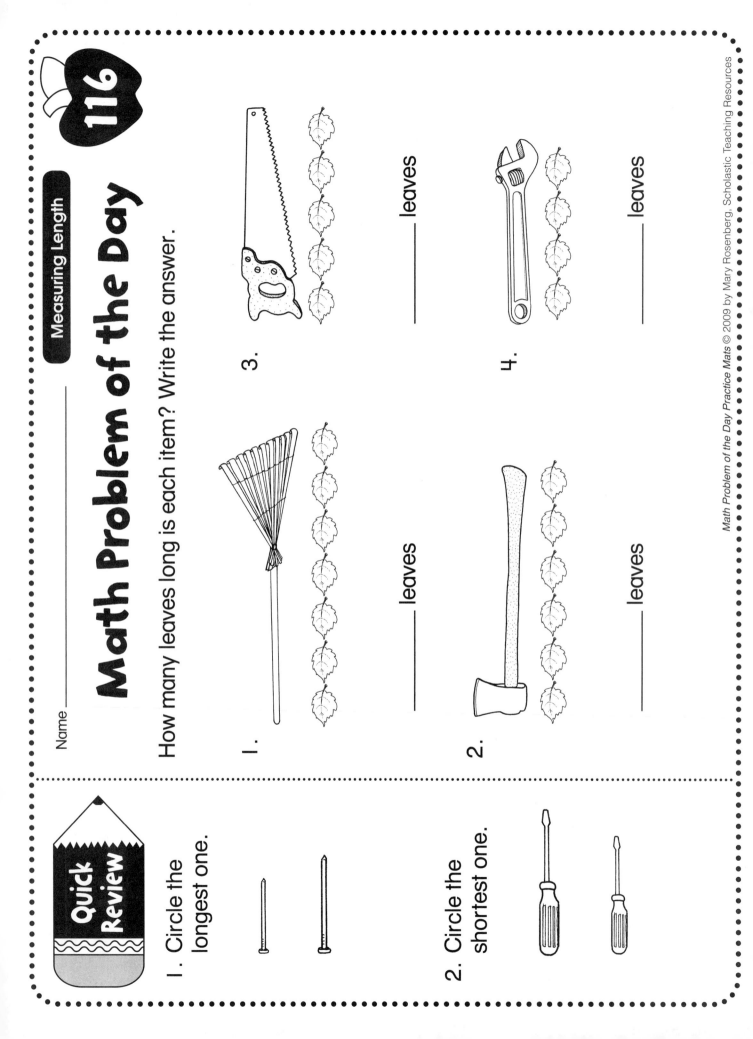

_____ leaves

2.

_____ leaves

3.

_____ leaves

4.

_____ leaves

Quick Review

1. Circle the longest one.

2. Circle the shortest one.

Name _____

Math Problem of the Day

Measuring Length

Measuring Length

How many teeth long is each item? Write the answer.

1. TOOTHPASTE

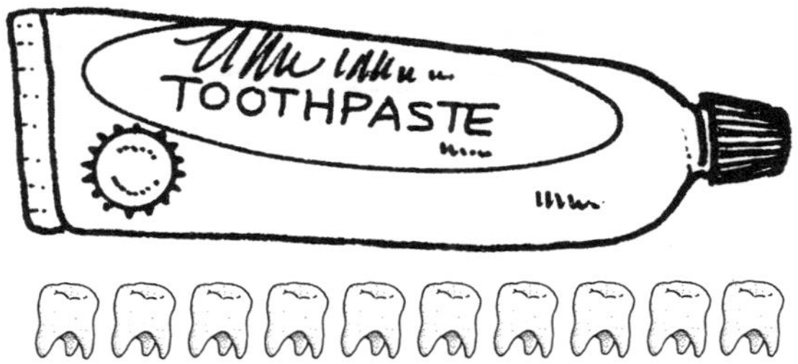

_____ teeth

2.

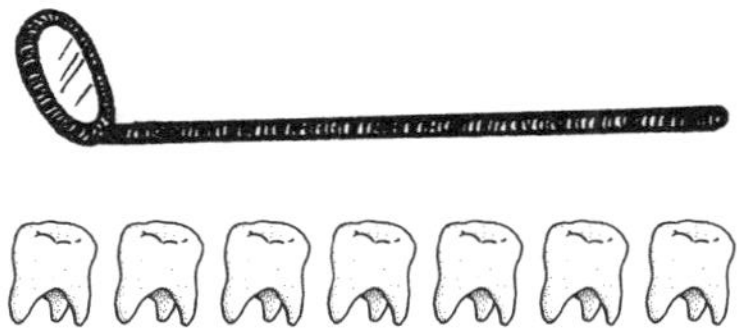

_____ teeth

3. Dental Floss

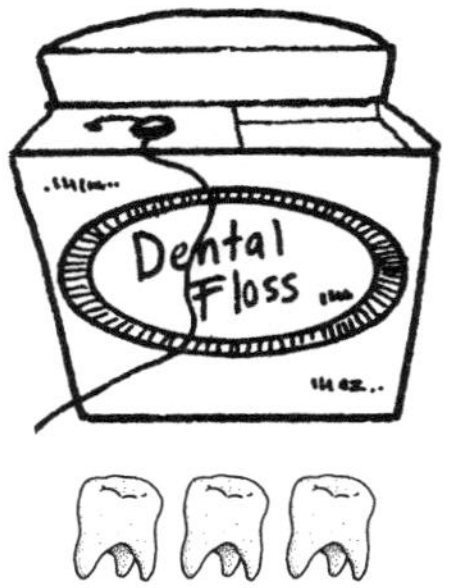

_____ teeth

4.

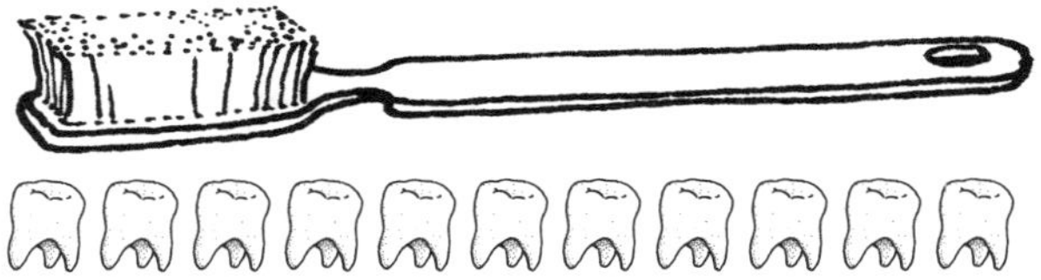

_____ teeth

Quick Review

1. Circle the shortest one.

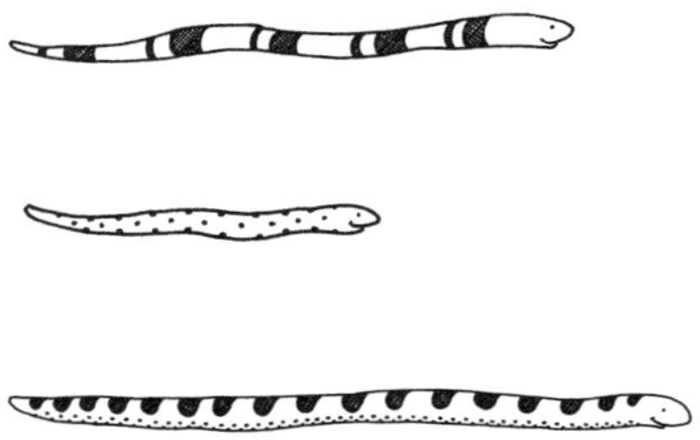

2. Circle the longest one.

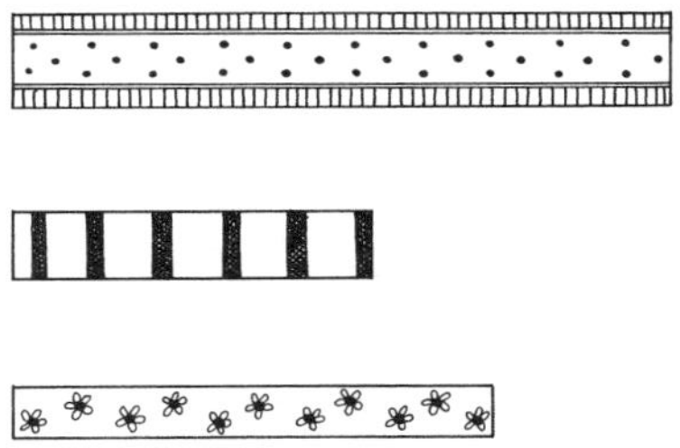

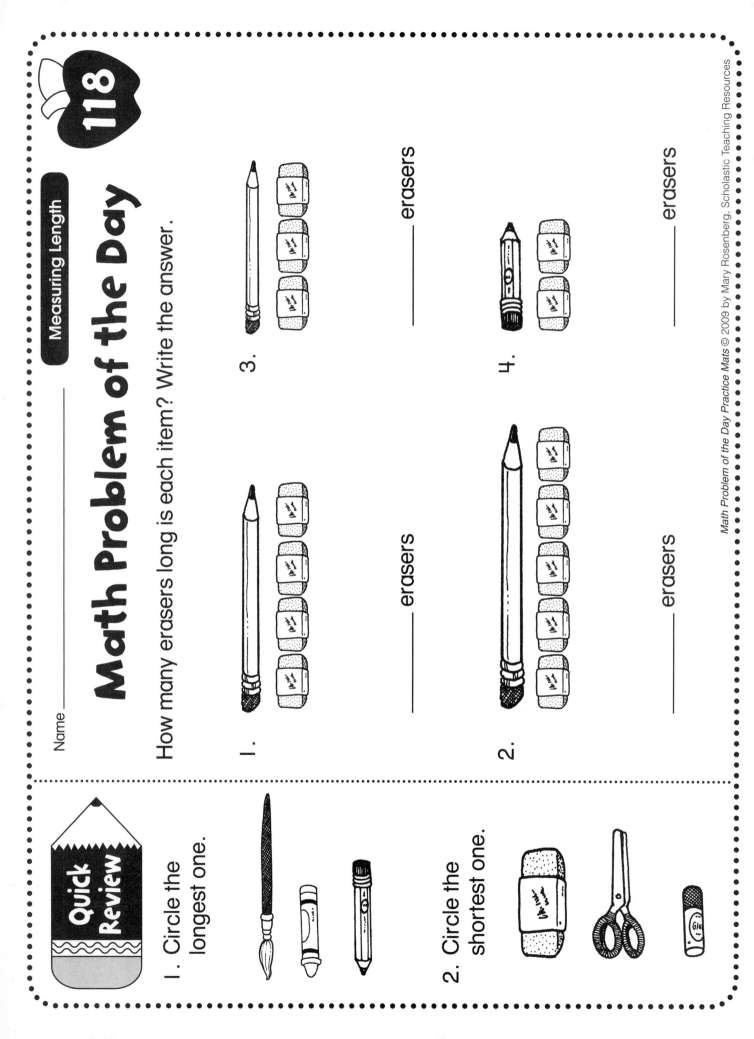

Name _____

Measuring Length

Math Problem of the Day

How many erasers long is each item? Write the answer.

1. _____ erasers

2. _____ erasers

3. _____ erasers

4. _____ erasers

Quick Review

1. Circle the longest one.

2. Circle the shortest one.

118

Math Problem of the Day Practice Mats © 2009 by Mary Rosenberg, Scholastic Teaching Resources

Math Problem of the Day

Name _____

How many inches long is each item? Write the answer.

1.

inches _____

2.

_____ inches

3.

_____ inches

4.

_____ inches

Quick Review

1. How much longer is rope A than rope B?

A

B

_____ inches longer

2. How much shorter is pencil B than pencil A?

A

B

_____ inches shorter

Name _____

Math Problem of the Day

How many inches tall is each item? Write the answer.

1. _____ inches tall

2. _____ inches tall

3. _____ inches tall

Quick Review

1. Circle the tallest one.

2. Circle the shortest one.

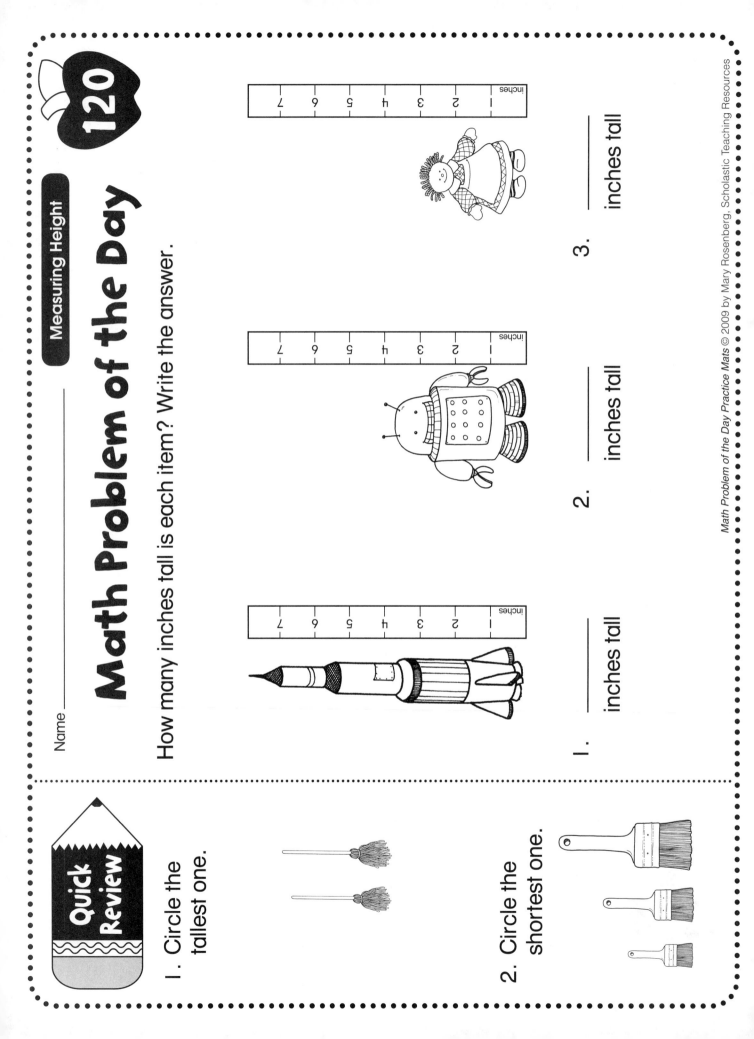

Name _____

Math Problem of the Day

Use the calendar to answer the questions.

Sunday	Monday	Tuesday	Wednesday	Thursday	Friday	Saturday
1	2	3	4	5	6	7
8	9	10	11	12	13	14
15	16	17	18	19	20	21
22	23	24	25	26	27	28
29	30					

1. How many days in one week? _____

2. What is the first day of the week? _____

3. What is the last day of the week? _____

4. How many days are in this month? _____

Quick Review

Write the time to the hour.

1.

_____:_____

2.

_____:_____

3.

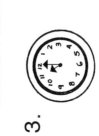

_____:_____

4.

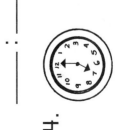

_____:_____

Name _____

Math Problem of the Day

Use the calendar to answer the questions.

Sunday	Monday	Tuesday	Wednesday	Thursday	Friday	Saturday
		1	2	3	4	5
6	7	8	9	10	11	12
13	14	15	16	17	18	19
20	21	22	23	24	25	26
27	28	29	30	31		

1. What day of the week does this month begin on? _____

2. What day of the week does this month end on? _____

3. How many day are in this month? _____

4. How many Saturdays are in this month? _____

Quick Review

Write the time to the half hour.

1. _____ : _____

2. _____ : _____

3. _____ : _____

4. _____ : _____

123

Using a Calendar

Math Problem of the Day

Fill in the missing numbers on the calendar. Answer the questions.

Sunday	Monday	Tuesday	Wednesday	Thursday	Friday	Saturday
			1	2		
5					10	
		14				18
19				23		
	27		29		31	

1. What day does this month begin on? _____

2. How many days are in this month? _____

3. What day of the week is the 20th? _____

4. How many Wednesdays are in this month? _____

Quick Review

Draw the hour hand on each clock.

1.  3:00

2.  5:00

3.  9:00

4.  10:00

Math Problem of the Day

Name _____

Fill in the calendar for the current month. Answer the questions.

Name of the month: _____

Sunday	Monday	Tuesday	Wednesday	Thursday	Friday	Saturday

1. How many days are in this month? _____

2. How many Mondays are in this month? _____

3. How many Saturdays are in this month? _____

4. What is the last day in this month? _____

Quick Review

Draw the hour hand on each clock.

1. 3:30

2. 7:30

3. 4:30

4. 6:30

Math Problem of the Day Practice Mats © 2009 by Mary Rosenberg, Scholastic Teaching Resources

Name _____

Math Problem of the Day

Using a Calendar

Use the calendar to answer the questions.

February

Sunday	Monday	Tuesday	Wednesday	Thursday	Friday	Saturday
						1
2 Groundhog Day	3	4	5	6	7	8 Soccer Practice
9	10	11	12 Piano Lesson	13	14 Valentine's Day	15
16	17	18 Grandma's Birthday	19	20	21	22
23	24	25	26	27	28	

1. When is Grandma's birthday? _____

2. What happens on the 8th? _____

3. When is Valentine's Day? _____

4. What happens on the first Sunday? _____

Quick Review

Draw the hands on each clock to show the time.

1. 4:00
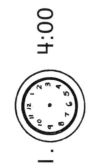

2. 9:30

3. 11:30

4. 1:00

Name _____

Math Problem of the Day

Adding Coins

126

Draw a picture to solve the word problem.

Jenny had 10¢. Her grandmother gave her 5 pennies. How much money does Jenny have now?

_____ ¢

Quick Review

Compare the value of the coins. Write >, <, or = on each line.

1. 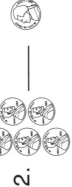 _____

2.  _____

3. _____

Math Problem of the Day Practice Mats © 2009 by Mary Rosenberg, Scholastic Teaching Resources

Name _____

Math Problem of the Day

Priscilla has 10¢.

Circle the combination of coins that Priscilla has.

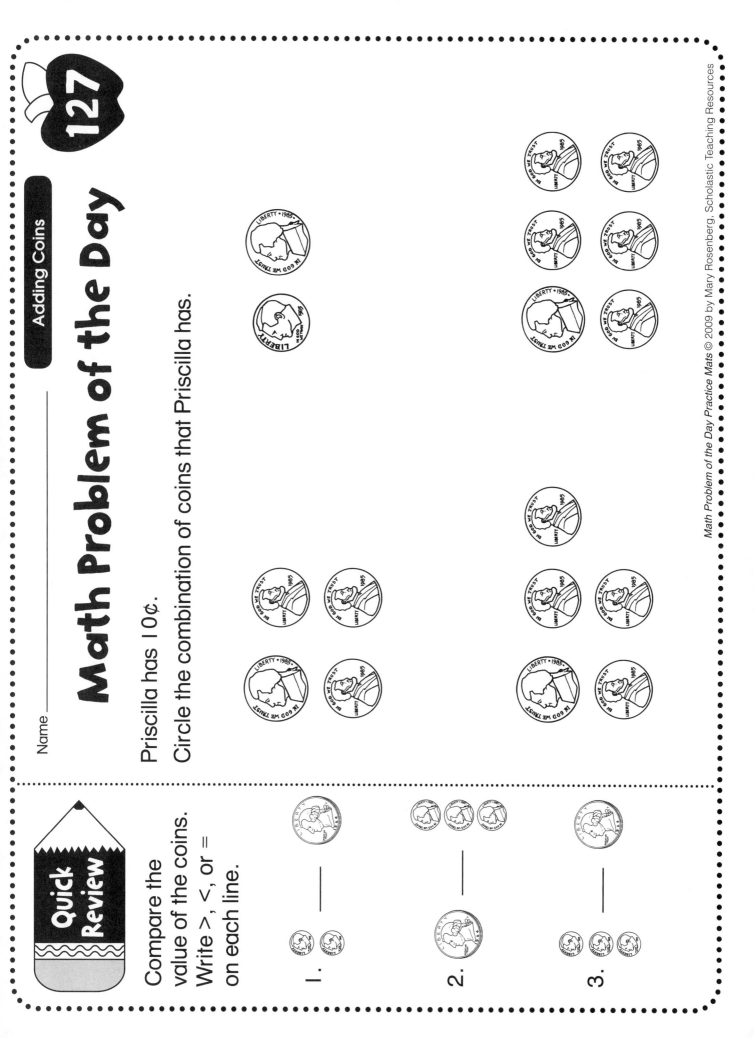

Quick Review

Compare the value of the coins. Write >, <, or = on each line.

1. _____

2. _____

3. _____

Name _____

Math Problem of the Day

Tom had five pennies, a dime, and two nickels in his piggy bank.

How much money was in his piggy bank?

Draw the coins to help you find the answer.

_____ ¢

Quick Review

Compare the value of the coins. Write >, <, or = on each line.

1.

2.

3.

Adding Coins

Name _____

Math Problem of the Day

Larry has two dimes. What can he buy with his money?
Circle the answer.

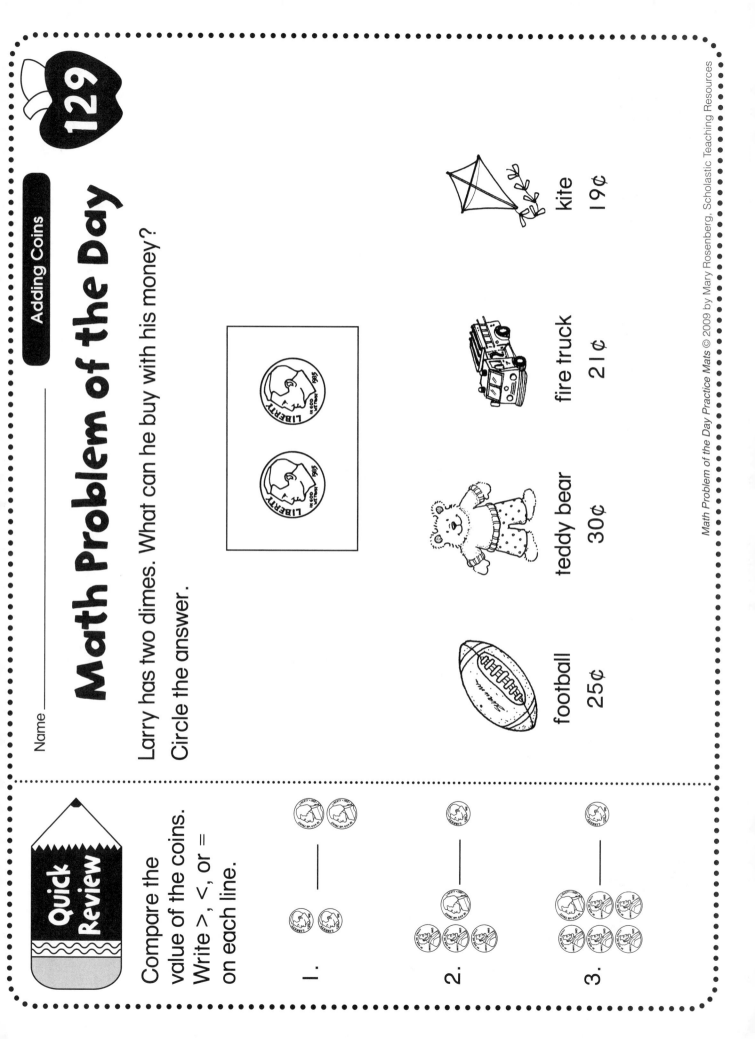

football   teddy bear   fire truck   kite
25¢   30¢   21¢   19¢

Quick Review

Compare the value of the coins. Write >, <, or = on each line.

1.

2.

3.

Name _____

Math Problem of the Day

Adding Money

Yummy Foods Menu

hamburger 25¢   taco 10¢   soup 15¢

pizza 20¢   salad 15¢   spaghetti 25¢

How much will each order cost? Write the answer.

1. taco and salad _____ ¢

2. two slices of pizza _____ ¢

3. hamburger and soup _____ ¢

4. spaghetti and salad _____ ¢

Math Problem of the Day Practice Mats © 2009 by Mary Rosenberg, Scholastic Teaching Resources

Quick Review

Compare the value of the coins. Write >, <, or = on each line.

1.

2.

3.

Name _____

Math Problem of the Day

Use the graph to answer the questions.

snake	🐍	🐍	🐍	🐍	🐍	🐍	🐍		
fish	🐟	🐟	🐟						
bird	🐦	🐦	🐦	🐦					
	1	2	3	4	5	6	7	8	9

1. How many of each animal?

snakes: _____   fish: _____   birds: _____

2. Are there more snakes or birds? _____

4. How many animals in all? _____

Math Problem of the Day Practice Mats © 2009 by Mary Rosenberg, Scholastic Teaching Resources

Quick Review

Count the ants.

1. _____

2. _____

3. _____

4. _____

Name _____

Math Problem of the Day

Use the graph to answer the questions.

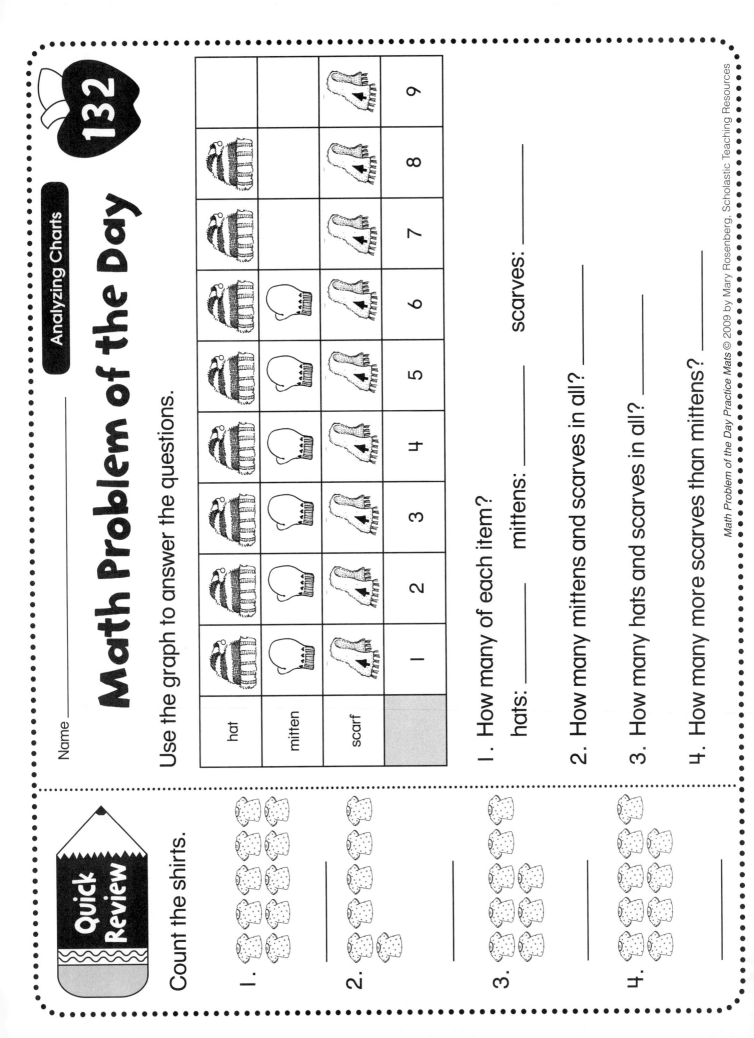

	1	2	3	4	5	6	7	8	9
hat		hat	hat	hat	hat	hat	hat	hat	
mitten	mitten	mitten	mitten	mitten	mitten	mitten			
scarf	scarf	scarf	scarf	scarf	scarf	scarf	scarf	scarf	scarf

1. How many of each item?

   hats: _____   mittens: _____   scarves: _____

2. How many mittens and scarves in all? _____

3. How many hats and scarves in all? _____

4. How many more scarves than mittens? _____

Quick Review

Count the shirts.

1. _____

2. _____

3. _____

4. _____

Math Problem of the Day

Name _____

Use the graph to answer the questions.

	1	2	3	4	5	6	7	8	9
rabbit	🐰	🐰	🐰						
mouse	🐭	🐭	🐭	🐭	🐭	🐭			
skunk	🦨	🦨	🦨	🦨					

1. How many of each animal?

   rabbits: _____   mice: _____   skunks: _____

2. How many more mice than rabbits? _____

3. How many more skunks than rabbits? _____

4. How many mice and skunks? _____

Quick Review

Write the number.

1. ⩍⩍⩍ _____

2. ⩍⩍⩍ ⩍⩍⩍ _____

3. ⩍⩍⩍ ⩍⩍⩍ ⩍⩍⩍ ||| _____

4. ⩍⩍⩍ || _____

Math Problem of the Day

Name _____

Complete the graph. Color a box for each car and truck.

	1	2	3	4	5	6	7	8	9
(car)									
(truck)									

1. How many trucks? _____ How many cars? _____

How many in all? Write a number sentence.

_____

2. How many more cars than trucks? Write a number sentence.

_____

Quick Review

Write the number.

1. ‖‖‖ | _____

2. ‖‖‖ ‖‖‖ _____

3. ‖‖‖ ‖‖‖ || _____

4. ‖‖‖ ‖‖‖ ‖‖‖ _____

Name _____

Math Problem of the Day

Complete the graph. Color a box for each item.

								9
							8	
						7		
					6			
				5				
			4					
		3						
	2							
1								

1. How many?

   hats: _____ shorts: _____ shirts: _____

2. How many in all? _____

3. How many more hats than shorts? Write a number sentence.

   _____

Quick Review

Count the items.

1. _____

2. _____

3. _____

Using Graphs

Math Problem of the Day

Complete the graph. Color a box for each ball.

	1	2	3	4	5	6	7	8	9

1. How many balls in all? _____

2. How many more footballs than baseballs? Write a number sentence.

3. How many fewer footballs than basketballs? Write a number sentence.

_____

Name _____

Quick Review

Count the items.

1.

2. _____

3. _____

Name _____

Math Problem of the Day

Complete the graph. Color a box for each animal.

🐖									
🐄									
🐔									
	1	2	3	4	5	6	7	8	9

1. There are five of which animal? Circle the answer.

2. How many more cows than pigs? _____

3. How many more cows than hens? _____

Quick Review

Count the items.

1. _____

2. _____

3. _____

Using Graphs

Math Problem of the Day

Name _____

Complete the graph. Color a box for each item.

			9
		8	
	7		
	6		
	5		
4			
3			
2			
1			

1. How many more turtles than dogs? Write a number sentence.

_____

2. How many dogs and cats? Write a number sentence.

_____

Math Problem of the Day Practice Mats © 2009 by Mary Rosenberg, Scholastic Teaching Resources

Quick Review

Write the number.

1. |||| |||| || _____

2. |||| |||| | _____

3. |||| |||| |||| |||| _____

4. |||| |||| |||| || _____

Name _____

Using Graphs

Math Problem of the Day

Complete the graph. Color a box for each item.

	1	2	3	4	5	6	7	8	9
🍭									
🍦									
🧁									

1. How many more lollipops than cupcakes? Write a number sentence.

_____

2. How many lollipops and ice cream cones? Write a number sentence.

_____

Math Problem of the Day Practice Mats © 2009 by Mary Rosenberg, Scholastic Teaching Resources

Quick Review

Write the number.

1. _____

2. _____

3. _____

Name _____

Math Problem of the Day

Use the tally marks to complete the graph. Color a box for each animal.

🐕 = ||| ꒐꒐꒐꒐꒐   🐈 = || ꒐꒐꒐꒐꒐

🐕								
🐈								
	1	2	3	4	5	6	7	8	9

1. How many dogs? _____ How many cats? _____

2. How many dogs and cats? Write a number sentence.
_____

3. How many more dogs than cats? Write a number sentence.
_____

Write the number.

1. ꒐꒐꒐꒐꒐ || _____

2. ||| _____

3. ꒐꒐꒐꒐꒐ ꒐꒐꒐꒐꒐ | _____

4. ꒐꒐꒐꒐꒐ ꒐꒐꒐꒐꒐ |
꒐꒐꒐꒐꒐ ꒐꒐꒐꒐꒐ | _____

Using Graphs

Math Problem of the Day

Name _____

Use the tally marks to complete the graph. Color a box for each item.

= ||||

= |||| ||||

= |||| |||

= |||| |

									9
								8	
							7		
						6			
					5				
				4					
			3						
		2							
	1								

1. How many fewer caps than crowns? Write a number sentence.

_____

2. How many more helmets than caps? Write a number sentence.

_____

3. How many items in all? _____

Quick Review

Write the number.

1. |||| |||| ||||
   |||| ||||

   _____

2. |||| ||||
   |||| |||

   _____

3. |||| |||| ||||
   |||| |||| ||

   _____

Math Problem of the Day

Name _____

Complete the graph. Color a box for each item.

🐻 = 2   🐻 = 5   🐻 = 8

🐻								
🐻								
🐻								
🐻								
1	2	3	4	5	6	7	8	9

1. There are eight of which bear? Circle the answer.

🐻   🐻   🐻

2. How many bears in all? _____

3. How many more sleeping bears than sitting bears? _____

Math Problem of the Day Practice Mats © 2009 by Mary Rosenberg, Scholastic Teaching Resources

Quick Review

Solve each pair of problems.

1. $2 + 7 =$ _____

$7 + 2 =$ _____

3. $5 + 3 =$ _____

$3 + 5 =$ _____

3. $1 + 6 =$ _____

$6 + 1 =$ _____

Math Problem of the Day

Name _____

Ask ten classmates to pick their favorite color.

Color a box for each answer.

	1	2	3	4	5	6	7	8	9	10
blue										
purple										
red										

1. How many people liked each color?

   blue: _____ purple: _____ red: _____

2. Do more people like blue or red? _____

3. Do more people like red or purple? _____

4. Which color did the most people like? _____

Math Problem of the Day Practice Mats © 2009 by Mary Rosenberg, Scholastic Teaching Resources

Quick Review

Solve each pair of problems.

1. 6 + 4 = _____

   4 + 6 = _____

2. 7 + 3 = _____

   3 + 7 = _____

3. 9 + 1 = _____

   1 + 9 = _____

Creating Graphs

Math Problem of the Day

Name _____

Ask ten classmates to pick their favorite food.

Color a box for each answer.

	1	2	3	4	5	6	7	8	9	10
pizza										
soup										
taco										

1. Which food did most people pick? Circle the answer.

2. Which food did the fewest people pick? Circle the answer.

3. How many people picked each food?

Quick Review

Find the sum.
Write a number sentence.

1.

_____

2.

_____

Math Problem of the Day Practice Mats © 2009 by Mary Rosenberg, Scholastic Teaching Resources

Name _____

Math Problem of the Day

Pick ten classmates. Ask them what time they go to bed.
Color a box for each answer.

	1	2	3	4	5	6	7	8	9	10
8:00										
8:30										
9:00										

1. How many classmates go to bed at 8:00? _____

2. Do more classmates go to bed at 8:00 or 9:00? _____

3. How many classmates go to bed before 9:00? _____

Quick Review

Make tally marks for each number.

1. 13

2. 16

3. 20

4. 19

Math Problem of the Day

Name _____

Pick ten classmates. What kind of shirt is each person wearing?
Make tally marks for each kind. Then complete the graph.

solid color _____   striped _____   other _____

solid color										
striped										
other										
	1	2	3	4	5	6	7	8	9	10

1. Which kind of shirt are the most people wearing? Circle the answer.

   solid color   striped   other

2. Which kind of shirt are the fewest people wearing? _____

3. How many solid color and striped shirts? Write a number sentence.

   _____

Math Problem of the Day Practice Mats © 2009 by Mary Rosenberg, Scholastic Teaching Resources

Quick Review

Make tally marks for each number.

1. 11

2. 7

3. 4

4. 8

Name _____

Math Problem of the Day

Ask ten classmates to pick their favorite activity.

Make tally marks for each answer. Then complete the graph.

jump rope _____   play sports _____   swing _____

jump rope									
play sports									
swing									
	1	2	3	4	5	6	7	8	9	10

1. What do the most classmates like to do? Circle the answer.

   jump rope   play sports   swing

2. Do more classmates like to jump rope or swing? _____

3. How many classmates like to play sports and jump rope?

   Write a number sentence. _____

Quick Review

Make tally marks for each number.

1. 10

2. 15

3. 9

4. 12

Name _____

Math Problem of the Day

148

Pick ten classmates. Ask them if they have pets or not.
Make tally marks for each answer. Then complete the graph.

pets _____   no pets _____

pets									
no pets									
	1	2	3	4	5	6	7	8	9	10

1. How many classmates in each group?

   pets: _____   no pets: _____

2. Which group has the most classmates? Circle the answer.

   pets   no pets

3. Use the graph to write a subtraction problem.

   _____

Math Problem of the Day Practice Mats © 2009 by Mary Rosenberg, Scholastic Teaching Resources

Quick Review

Write the missing number.

1. 6 + 7 = _____

   _____ − 7 = 6

3. 8 + 3 = _____

   _____ − 3 = 8

3. 9 + 4 = _____

   _____ − 4 = 9

4. 5 + 7 = _____

   _____ − 7 = 5

Name _____

Creating Graphs

Math Problem of the Day

Ask ten classmates if they would rather be a frog or a turtle.
Color a box for each answer.

10		
9		
8		
7		
6		
5		
4		
3		
2		
1		
	frog	turtle

1. Which would more classmates like to be? Circle the answer.

2. How many classmates would like to be a frog? _____

3. How many classmates would like to be a turtle? _____

4. Use the graph to write a subtraction problem.

_____

Math Problem of the Day Practice Mats © 2009 by Mary Rosenberg, Scholastic Teaching Resources

Quick Review

Look at the bats. Answer the questions.

How many of each?

bats _____

wings _____

eyes _____

legs _____

ears _____

heads _____

Math Problem of the Day

150

Name _____

Ask ten classmates if they would rather be a spider or a butterfly.
Color a box for each answer.

1. Which would more classmates like to be? Circle the answer.

2. How many classmates would like to be a spider? _____

3. How many classmates would like to be a butterfly? _____

10		
9		
8		
7		
6		
5		
4		
3		
2		
1		
	spider	butterfly

Quick Review

Look at the spiders. Answer the questions.

How many of each?

eyes _____

spiders _____

legs _____

bodies _____

heads _____

Math Problem of the Day

Name _____

Ask ten classmates which shape they like best.
Color a box for each answer.

10			
9			
8			
7			
6			
5			
4			
3			
2			
1			
	☆ star	♡ heart	⬅ arrow

1. Which shape do most classmates like best? Circle the answer.

   ☆   ♡   ⬅

2. Which shape had the fewest votes? Circle the answer.

   ☆   ♡   ⬅

3. Use the graph to write a subtraction problem.

   _____

Quick Review

Look at the hippos. Answer the questions.

How many of each?

ears _____

noses _____

legs _____

eyes _____

feet _____

Math Problem of the Day

Creating Graphs

Name _____

Ask ten classmates which weather they like best.
Color a box for each answer.

	sunny	windy	rainy	snowy
10				
9				
8				
7				
6				
5				
4				
3				
2				
1				

1. Which kind of weather do most classmates like? Circle the answer.

2. Which kind of weather do the fewest classmates like? Circle the answer.

Quick Review

Look at the cows. Answer the questions.

How many of each?

eyes _____

legs _____

spots _____

noses _____

ears _____

tails _____

Math Problem of the Day Practice Mats © 2009 by Mary Rosenberg, Scholastic Teaching Resources

Math Problem of the Day

Name _____

Flip a penny ten times. Color a box each time to show how the penny landed. Then answer the questions.

10		
9		
8		
7		
6		
5		
4		
3		
2		
1		
	heads	tails

1. How many times did the penny land on each side?

heads _____   tails _____

2. Which side did the penny land on the most? Circle the answer.

3. Use the graph to write a subtraction problem.

_____

Quick Review

Look at the ladybugs. Answer the questions.

How many of each?

legs _____

wings _____

spots _____

antennae _____

heads _____

Name _____

Math Problem of the Day

Use a paper clip and pencil to work the spinners below.
Use the spinners to help you answer the questions.

Green | Yellow

A

Green

Yellow

B

Green

Yellow

C

1. Which spinner would you use to land mostly on each color?

Write the letter for each spinner on the line.

green: _____   yellow: _____

2. Which spinner would you use to land equally on yellow and green?

Circle the answer: A   B   C

Quick Review

Write the answer.

1. 9 – 2 = _____

2. 9 – 3 = _____

3. 9 – 4 = _____

4. 9 – 5 = _____

5. 9 – 6 = _____

6. 9 – 7 = _____

Applying Concepts of Probability

Math Problem of the Day

Name _____

Use red and blue to
color the spinner.
Color it so that the
spinner will land most
often on blue.

1. Use a paper clip and pencil to work the spinner.
Spin the spinner ten times. Record the results.

red									
blue									

2. How many times did the spinner land on each color?

red: _____   blue: _____

Math Problem of the Day Practice Mats © 2009 by Mary Rosenberg, Scholastic Teaching Resources

Quick Review

Write the answer.

1. $11 - 9 =$ _____

2. $11 - 8 =$ _____

3. $11 - 7 =$ _____

4. $11 - 6 =$ _____

5. $11 - 5 =$ _____

6. $11 - 4 =$ _____

Math Problem of the Day

Name _____

Design a spinner that would have an equal chance of landing on red and yellow.

1. Use a paper clip and pencil to work the spinner. Spin the spinner ten times. Record the results.

red	
yellow	

2. How many times did the spinner land on each color?

red: _____ yellow: _____

Math Problem of the Day Practice Mats © 2009 by Mary Rosenberg, Scholastic Teaching Resources

Quick Review

Write the answer.

1. $15 - 7 =$ _____

2. $15 - 8 =$ _____

3. $15 - 9 =$ _____

4. $15 - 6 =$ _____

5. $15 - 5 =$ _____

6. $15 - 10 =$ _____

Name _____

Math Problem of the Day

Answer the questions about the diagram.

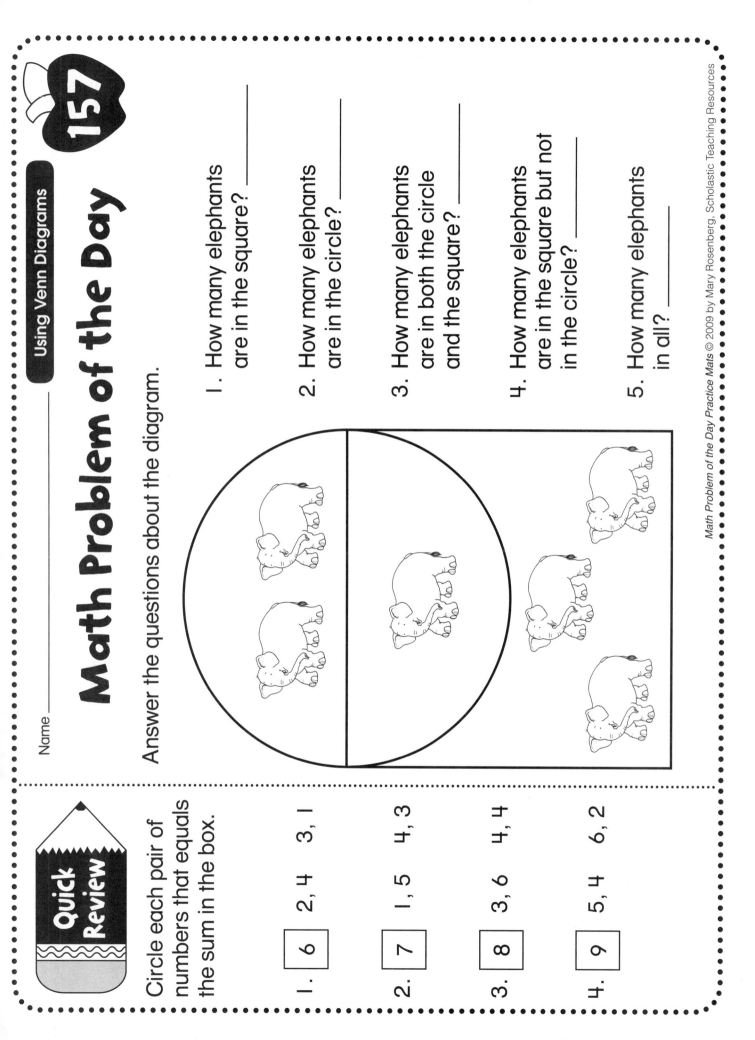

1. How many elephants are in the square? _____

2. How many elephants are in the circle? _____

3. How many elephants are in both the circle and the square? _____

4. How many elephants are in the square but not in the circle? _____

5. How many elephants in all? _____

Math Problem of the Day Practice Mats © 2009 by Mary Rosenberg, Scholastic Teaching Resources

Quick Review

Circle each pair of numbers that equals the sum in the box.

1. ☐ 6   2, 4   3, 1

2. ☐ 7   1, 5   4, 3

3. ☐ 8   3, 6   4, 4

4. ☐ 9   5, 4   6, 2

Name _____

Math Problem of the Day

Answer the questions about the diagram.

1. How many hats are in both the circle and the square? _____

2. How many hats are in the circle? _____

3. How many hats are in the square? _____

4. How many hats are in the circle but not in the square? _____

5. How many hats in all? _____

Quick Review

Circle each pair of numbers that equals the sum in the box.

1. | 4 | 1, 2   3, 1

2. | 6 | 2, 3   3, 3

3. | 9 | 7, 1   6, 3

4. | 8 | 5, 3   4, 2

Name _____

Math Problem of the Day

Answer the questions about the diagram.

1. How many pencils are in the circle? _____

2. How many crayons are in the square? _____

3. How many pencils are in the circle but not in the square? _____

4. Which item is in both the circle and the square? _____

5. How many items in all? _____

Quick Review

Circle each pair of numbers that equals the sum in the box.

1. $\boxed{10}$ 3, 6   5, 5

2. $\boxed{11}$ 7, 3   8, 3

3. $\boxed{12}$ 6, 5   5, 7

4. $\boxed{13}$ 9, 4   8, 3

Name _____

Math Problem of the Day

Using Venn Diagrams

160

Answer the questions about the diagram.

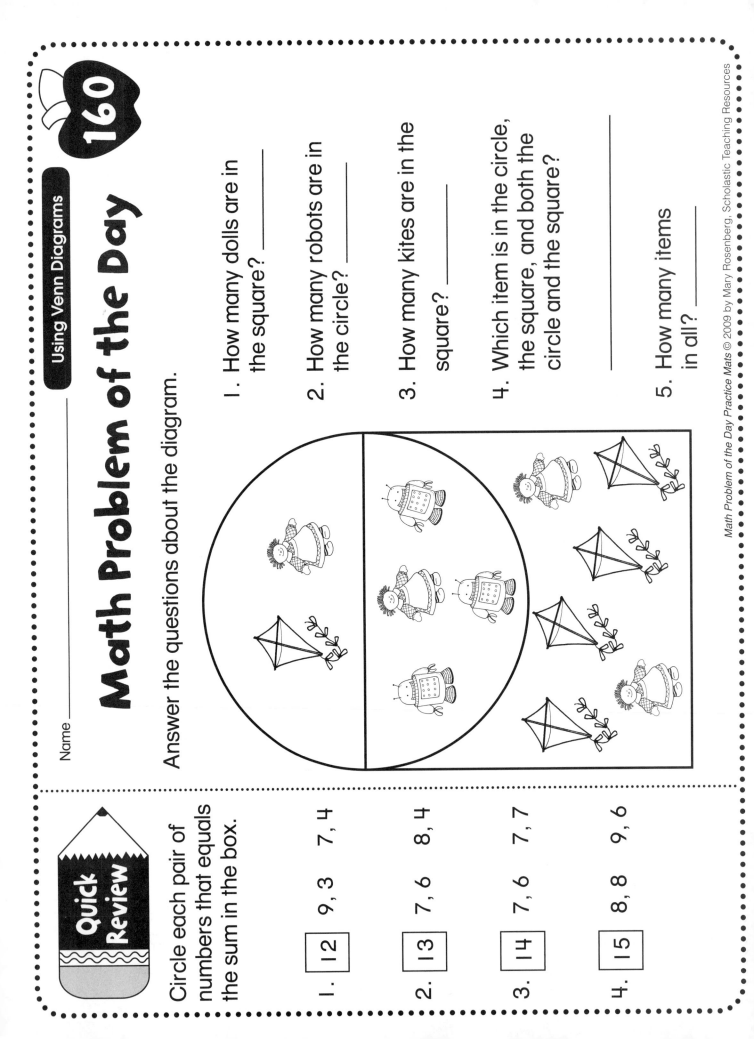

1. How many dolls are in the square? _____

2. How many robots are in the circle? _____

3. How many kites are in the square? _____

4. Which item is in the circle, the square, and both the circle and the square? _____

5. How many items in all? _____

Quick Review

Circle each pair of numbers that equals the sum in the box.

1. | 12 | 9, 3   7, 4

2. | 13 | 7, 6   8, 4

3. | 14 | 7, 6   7, 7

4. | 15 | 8, 8   9, 6

Math Problem of the Day Practice Mats © 2009 by Mary Rosenberg, Scholastic Teaching Resources

Math Problem of the Day

161

Answer the questions about the diagram.

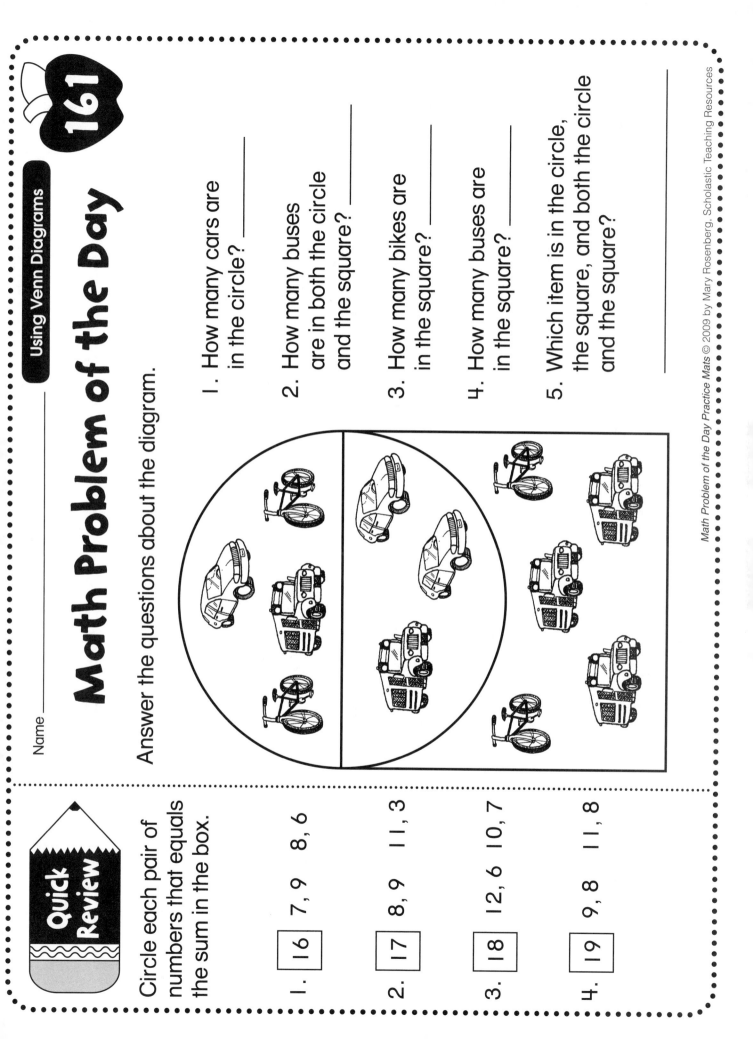

1. How many cars are in the circle? _____

2. How many buses are in both the circle and the square? _____

3. How many bikes are in the square? _____

4. How many buses are in the square? _____

5. Which item is in the circle, the square, and both the circle and the square? _____

Math Problem of the Day Practice Mats © 2009 by Mary Rosenberg, Scholastic Teaching Resources

Quick Review

Circle each pair of numbers that equals the sum in the box.

1. | 16 | 7, 9   8, 6

2. | 17 | 8, 9   11, 3

3. | 18 | 12, 6   10, 7

4. | 19 | 9, 8   11, 8

Name _____

Math Problem of the Day

Divide the pizza in half.

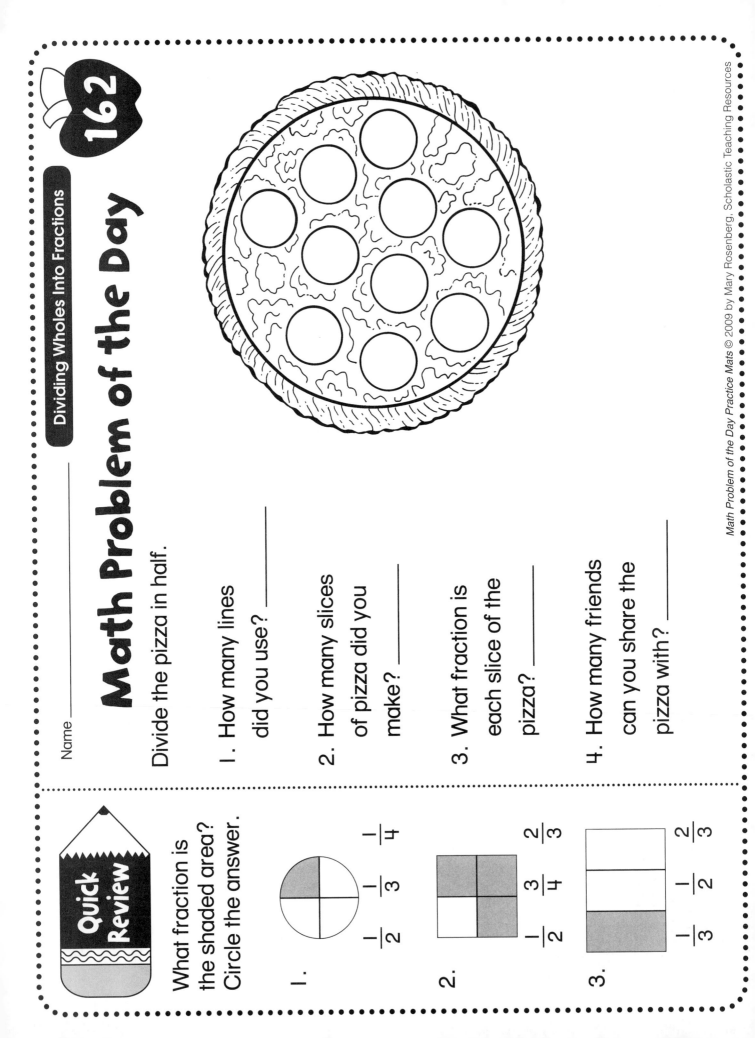

1. How many lines
did you use? _____

2. How many slices
of pizza did you
make? _____

3. What fraction is
each slice of the
pizza? _____

4. How many friends
can you share the
pizza with? _____

Quick Review

What fraction is
the shaded area?
Circle the answer.

1.

$\frac{1}{2}$ $\frac{1}{3}$ $\frac{1}{4}$

2.

$\frac{1}{2}$ $\frac{3}{4}$ $\frac{2}{3}$

3.

$\frac{1}{3}$ $\frac{1}{2}$ $\frac{2}{3}$

Math Problem of the Day

Name _____

Divide the hot dog into three equal parts.

1. How many lines did you use?

   _____

2. What fraction is each piece of the hot dog?

   _____

Divide the hot dog so that you can share it equally with three friends.

3. How many lines did you use?

   _____

4. What fraction is each piece of the hot dog?

   _____

Quick Review

What fraction is the shaded area? Circle the answer.

1. $\frac{2}{6}$ $\frac{3}{6}$ $\frac{4}{6}$

2. $\frac{1}{2}$ $\frac{1}{3}$ $\frac{1}{4}$

3. $\frac{1}{2}$ $\frac{1}{3}$ $\frac{1}{4}$

Quick Review

Answer the questions about the graph.

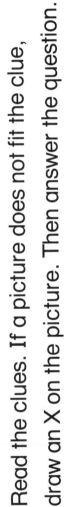

Pets Sold

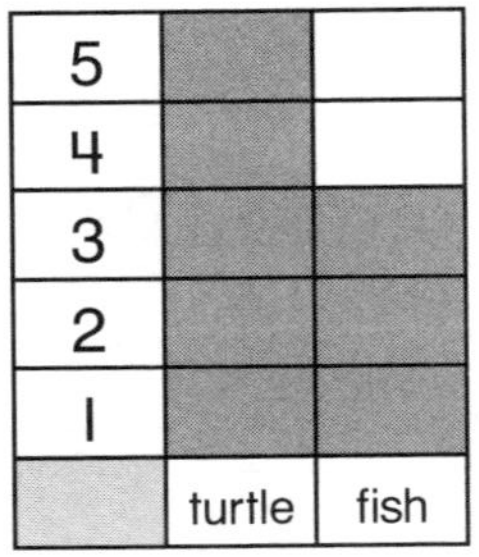

5
4
3
2
1
turtle
fish

1. How many fish were sold? ______
2. How many animals were sold in all? ______
3. Were more fish or turtles sold? ______

Name ____________________

Using Deductive Reasoning

Math Problem of the Day

164

Read the clues. If a picture does not fit the clue, draw an X on the picture. Then answer the question.

- I do not have wings.
- My body is made up of segments.
- I have 8 legs.

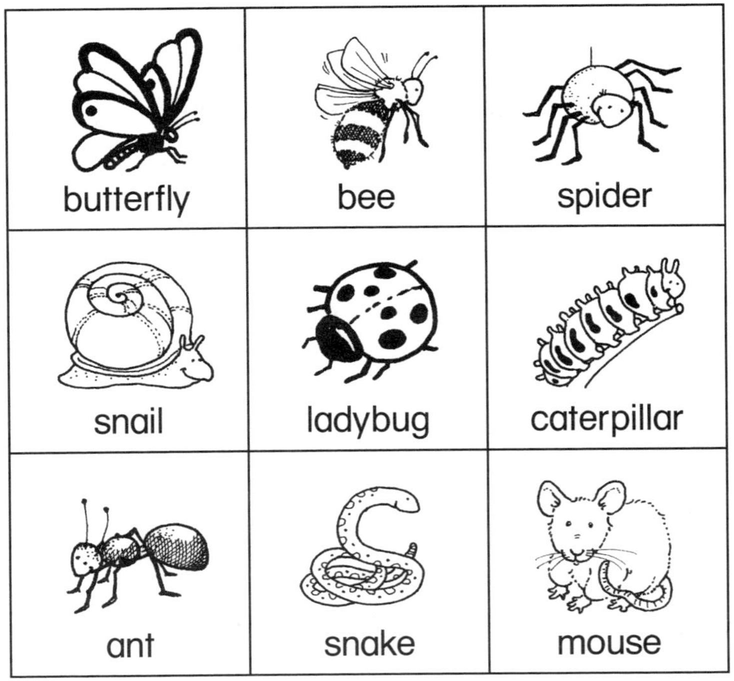

butterfly
bee
spider
snail
ladybug
caterpillar
ant
snake
mouse

Which critter am I?

____

Write a different clue about the critter.

____

Name _____

Math Problem of the Day

Read the clues. If a picture does not fit the clue,
draw an X on the picture. Then answer the question.

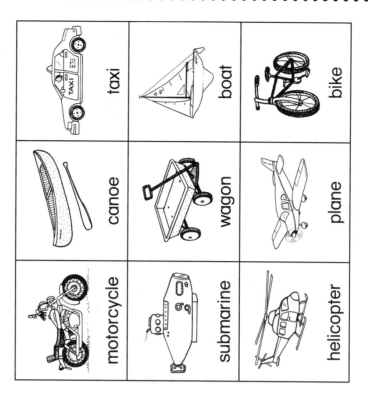

taxi	canoe	motorcycle
boat	wagon	submarine
bike	plane	helicopter

- I travel on land.

- I have 4 wheels.

- I do not have a motor.

Which vehicle am I ? _____

_____

Write a different clue
about the vehicle.

_____

Quick Review

Answer the questions
about the graph.

Absent Kids

	Mon.	Wed.	Fri.
5			
4			
3			
2			
1			

1. On which day
were the fewest
kids absent?

_____

2. How many kids
were absent in all?

_____

Name _____

166

Name _____

166

Using Deductive Reasoning

Math Problem of the Day

Use the clues to find the mystery child.

- I have short hair.

- I have something on my head.

- I am not a boy.

What is my name? _____

_____

Write a different clue about the mystery child.

_____

Quick Review

Answer the questions about the graph.

Favorite Color

10			
8			
6			
4			
2			
	red	blue	green

1. Which color did the fewest people like?

_____

2. How many more people like blue more than red?

_____

3. How many people voted? _____

Math Problem of the Day Practice Mats © 2009 by Mary Rosenberg, Scholastic Teaching Resources

Name

Math Problem of the Day

Use the clues to find the mystery fruit.

- I do not grow in bunches.

- I am red.

- My seeds grow on my skin.

Which fruit am I?

_____

Write a different clue
about the mystery fruit.

_____

pear	orange	grapes
cherries	pumpkin	strawberry
berries	apple	bananas

Quick Review

Answer the questions
about the graph.

Votes for President

25		
20		
15		
10		
5		
	Abe	Ben

1. How many people
   voted for each
   candidate?

   Abe: _____
   Ben: _____

2. Which candidate
   had the most
   votes? _____

Name _____

Math Problem of the Day

Use the clues to find the mystery animal.

kangaroo	gorilla	hippo
elephant	camel	monkey
tiger	leopard	armadillo

- I have fur.

- I can stand on two legs.

- I can leap long distances.

Which animal am I? _____

_____

Write a different clue
about the mystery animal.

_____

Quick Review

Answer the questions
about the graph.

Sports Fans

50		
40		
30		
20		
10		
	baseball	football

1. How many people
   like baseball? _____

2. How many people
   like football? _____

3. Use the graph to
   write a subtraction
   problem.

   _____

Quick Review

Answer the questions about the graph.

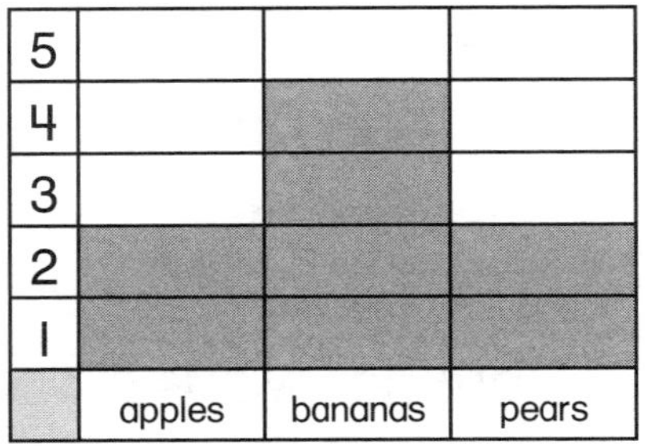

1. What type of item is shown on the graph? ________
2. How many of each?
   apples ______
   bananas ______
   pears ______
3. How many in all?
   ______

Name ______________________________

Comparing Attributes

Math Problem of the Day

169

Use the information shown below to answer the questions.

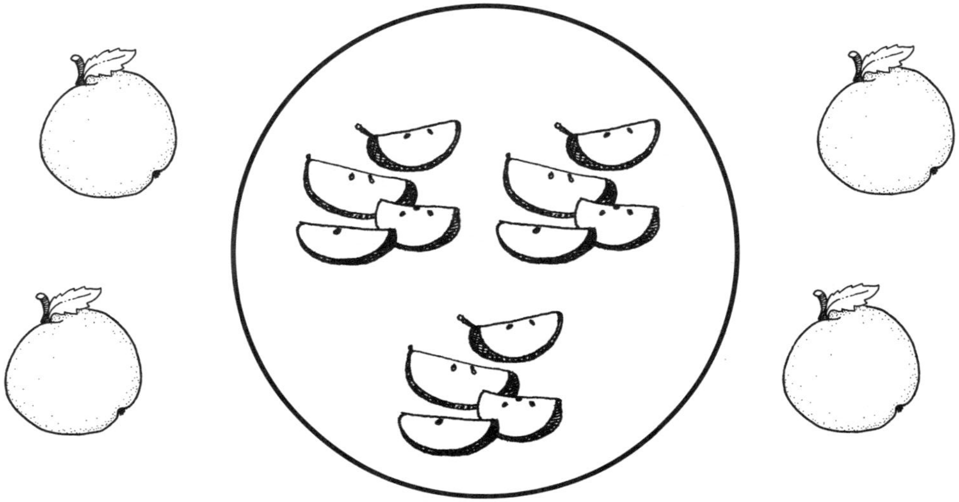

1. What do the apples in the circle have in common?

   ____

2. What do the apples outside the circle have in common?

   ____

3. How many apples and apple pieces in all? ____________________

Math Problem of the Day Practice Mats © 2009 by Mary Rosenberg, Scholastic Teaching Resources

Math Problem of the Day

Name _____

Use the information shown below to answer the questions.

1. What do the ties in the circle have in common?

   _____

2. What do the ties outside the circle have in common?

   _____

3. How many ties in all? _____

Quick Review

Answer the questions about the graph.

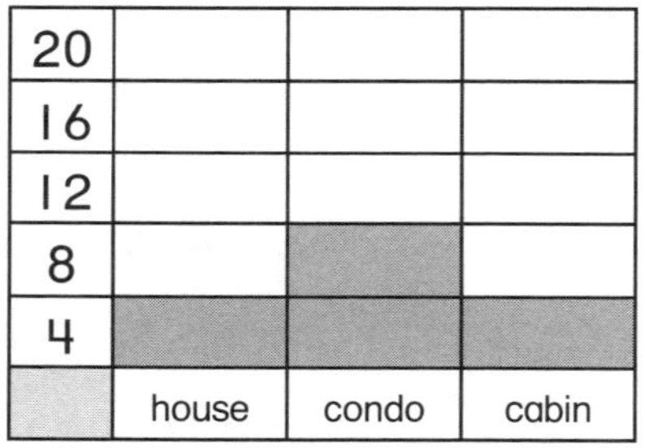

	house	condo	cabin
20			
16			
12			
8		▓	
4	▓	▓	▓

1. What type of item is shown on the graph? _____

2. How are the items counted?

   _____

3. How many of each?

   house _____

   condo _____

   cabin _____

Math Problem of the Day

Name _____

Use the information shown below to answer the questions.

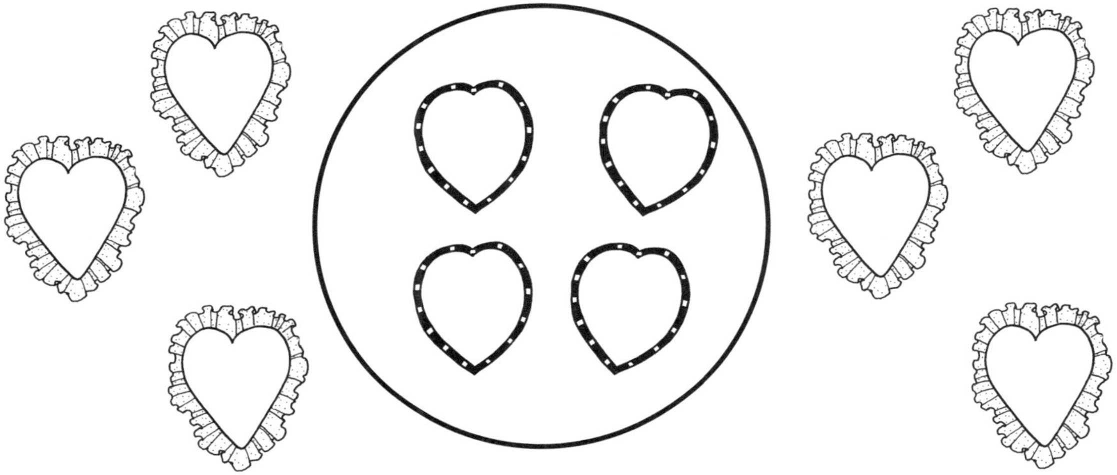

1. What do the hearts in the circle have in common?

_____

2. What do the hearts outside the circle have in common?

_____

3. How many hearts in all? _____

Quick Review

Answer the questions about the graph.

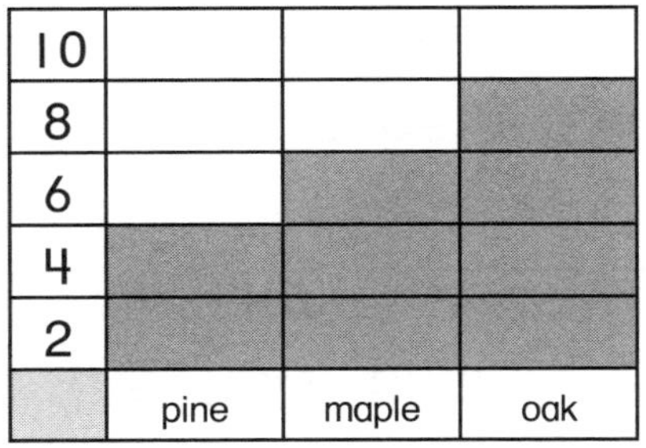

10			
8			oak
6		maple	
4			
2	pine		

1. What type of item is shown on the graph? _____

2. How are the items counted? _____

3. How many of each?

pine _____

maple _____

oak _____

Name _____

Math Problem of the Day

Use the information shown below to answer the questions.

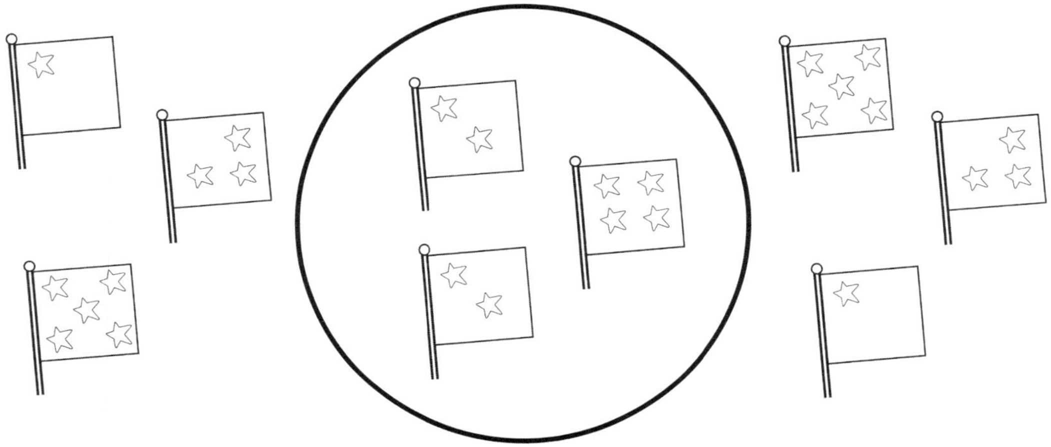

1. What do the flags in the circle have in common?

_____

2. What do the flags outside the circle have in common?

_____

3. What do all the flags have in common?

_____

Quick Review

Answer the questions about the graph.

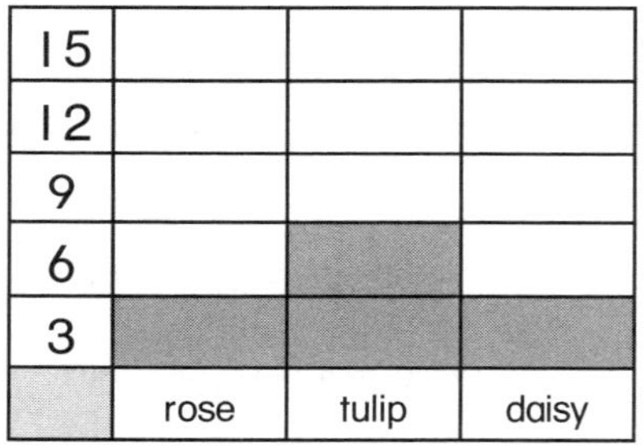

15			
12			
9			
6			
3			
	rose	tulip	daisy

1. What type of item is shown on the graph? _____

2. How are the items counted? _____

3. How many of each?

rose _____

tulip _____

daisy _____

173

Name _____

Math Problem of the Day

Use the information shown below to answer the questions.

1. What do the animals in the circle have in common?

   _____

2. What do the animals outside the circle have in common?

   _____

3. What do all the animals have in common?

   _____

Quick Review

Answer the questions about the graph.

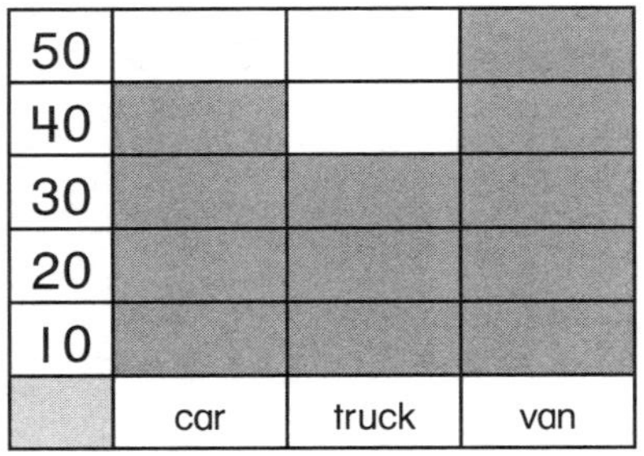

50			
40			
30			
20			
10			
	car	truck	van

1. What type of item is shown on the graph? _____

2. How are the items counted?

   _____

3. How many of each?

   car _____
   truck _____
   van _____

Name _____

Math Problem of the Day

Read the clues to discover where each child lives.
Write each child's name on the correct floor.

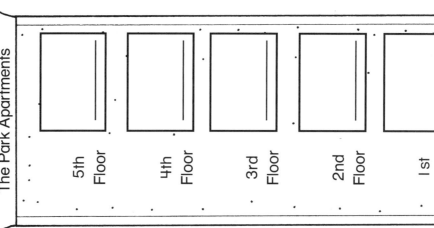

The Park Apartments
5th Floor
4th Floor
3rd Floor
2nd Floor
1st Floor

Gina   Lisa   Ann   Matt   Bob

- Matt lives on the top floor.

- Ann lives three floors below Matt.

- Gina lives two floors above Ann.

- Lisa lives on the 3rd floor.

- On what floor does Bob live? _____

Quick Review

Use each set of numbers to make two addition problems and two subtraction problems.

1. 1, 2, 3

___ + ___ = ___

___ + ___ = ___

___ − ___ = ___

___ − ___ = ___

2. 2, 3, 5

___ + ___ = ___

___ + ___ = ___

___ − ___ = ___

___ − ___ = ___

Math Problem of the Day

Name _____

Read the clues to discover where each child stood in line.
Write each child's name in the correct box.

Ned   Jen   Tim   Amy   Dan

- Amy was the line leader.

- Dan was last in line.

- Ned stood behind Amy and in front of Tim.

Where did Jen stand? _____

1st	2nd	3rd	4th	5th
___	___	___	___	___

Quick Review

Use each set of numbers to make two addition problems and two subtraction problems.

1. 3, 4, 7

___ + ___ = ___
___ + ___ = ___
___ − ___ = ___
___ − ___ = ___

2. 3, 5, 8

___ + ___ = ___
___ + ___ = ___
___ − ___ = ___
___ − ___ = ___

Using Graphic Organizers

Math Problem of the Day

Name _____

Read the clues to discover where each person lives.
Write each person's name under the correct house.

| 12 | 14 | 16 | 18 | 20 |

- Norma lives in house 16.

- Bert lives in house 12.

- Ron lives two houses to the right of Norma.

- Lee lives between Bert and Norma.

- Where does Candy live? _____

Quick Review

Use each set of numbers to make two addition problems and two subtraction problems.

1. 4, 5, 9

___ + ___ = ___

___ + ___ = ___

___ − ___ = ___

___ − ___ = ___

2. 3, 6, 9

___ + ___ = ___

___ + ___ = ___

___ − ___ = ___

___ − ___ = ___

Name _____

Math Problem of the Day

Using Graphic Organizers

177

Read the clues to discover which shape belongs to each person.

Write each person's name under the correct shape.

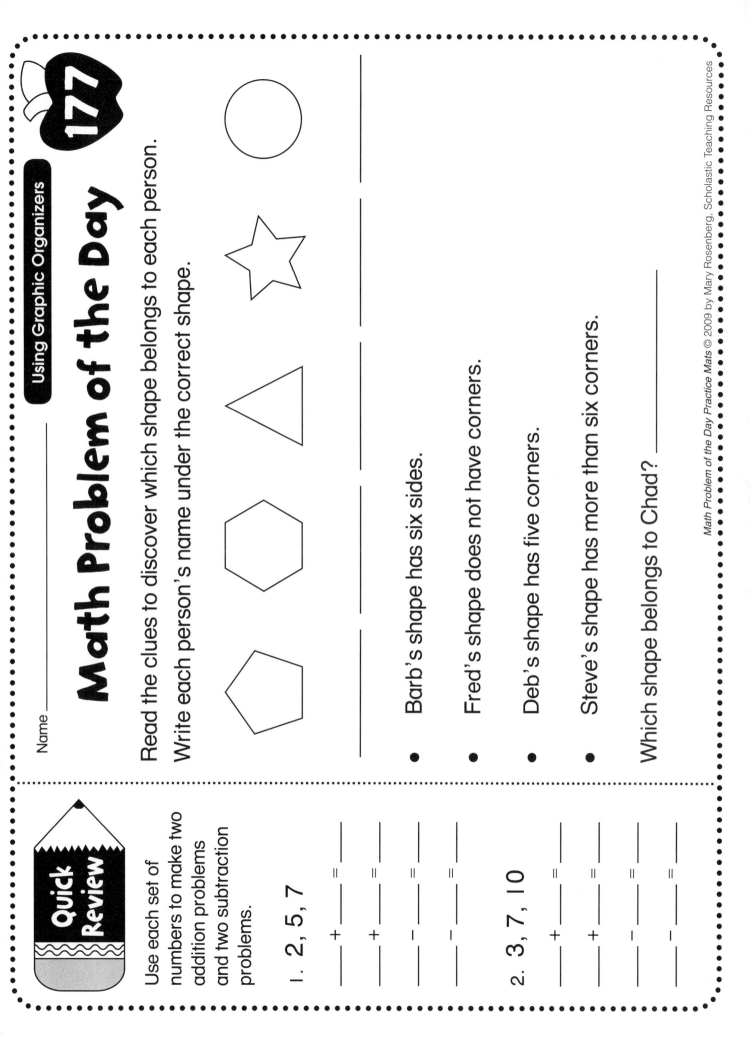

- Barb's shape has six sides.

- Fred's shape does not have corners.

- Deb's shape has five corners.

- Steve's shape has more than six corners.

Which shape belongs to Chad? _____

Quick Review

Use each set of numbers to make two addition problems and two subtraction problems.

1. 2, 5, 7

___ + ___ = ___

___ + ___ = ___

___ − ___ = ___

___ − ___ = ___

2. 3, 7, 10

___ + ___ = ___

___ + ___ = ___

___ − ___ = ___

___ − ___ = ___

Math Problem of the Day Practice Mats © 2009 by Mary Rosenberg, Scholastic Teaching Resources

Math Problem of the Day

Name _____

Read each clue. If the answer is no, make an X in the box.

If the answer is yes, make an O in the box.

Sasha			
Nicole			
Phil			

- Sasha does not wear helmets or tall hats.

- Phil wears only helmets.

- Nicole does not wear hats with straps or jewels.

Who wears each hat?
Write the name on the line.

_____

_____

_____

Quick Review

Circle the heavier item in each pair of pictures.

1.

2.

3.

4.

Name _____

Math Problem of the Day

Read each clue. If the answer is no, make an X in the box.
If the answer is yes, make an O in the box.

- Pat did not drink milk or water.

- Jim drank water.

- Betty did not drink fruit juice or water.

	MILK	[cup]	APPLE JUICE
Betty			
Jim			
Pat			

What did each person drink?
Write the name on the line.

[milk] _____

[cup] _____

[juice box] _____

Quick Review

Circle the heavier item in each pair of pictures.

1.

2.

3.

4.

Using Graphic Organizers

Math Problem of the Day

Name _____

Read each clue. If the answer is no, make an X in the box.

If the answer is yes, make an O in the box.

- Grace does not have curly or short hair.

- Brenda has curly hair.

- Stacy does not have long hair.

Write the name of each girl beside her picture.

_____

_____

_____

Brenda			
Grace			
Stacy			

Quick Review

Circle the lighter item in each pair of pictures.

1.

2.

3.

4.

Answer Key

Math Problem of the Day 1

1. $3 + 2 = 5$
2. $4 + 1 = 5$

Quick Review
1. 3   2. 2

Math Problem of the Day 2

1. $3 + 3 = 6$
2. $2 + 5 = 7$

Quick Review
1. 3   2. 3

Math Problem of the Day 3

1. $6 + 3 = 9$
2. $4 + 4 = 8$

Quick Review
1. 4   2. 7

Math Problem of the Day 4

1. $5 + 2 = 7$
2. $4 + 5 = 9$

Quick Review
1. 1   2. 9

Math Problem of the Day 5

1. $2 + 6 = 8$
2. $5 + 3 = 8$

Quick Review
1. 5   2. 3

Math Problem of the Day 6

1. 9   2. 9   3. 9
4. 7   5. 7   6. 10

Quick Review
1. Students should draw 3 circles.
2. Students should draw 7 circles.
3. Students should draw 5 circles.

Math Problem of the Day 7

1. 8   2. 9   3. 8
4. 10   5. 10   6. 4

Quick Review
1. Students should draw 2 squares.
2. Students should draw 8 squares.
3. Students should draw 4 squares.

Math Problem of the Day 8

1. 9   2. 8   3. 9
4. 7   5. 9   6. 4

Quick Review
1. Students should draw 1 triangle.
2. Students should draw 9 triangles.
3. Students should draw 6 triangles.

Math Problem of the Day 9

1. 10   2. 12   3. 11
4. 11   5. 12   6. 13

Quick Review
1. Students should draw 3 ovals.
2. Students should draw 2 ovals.
3. Students should draw 5 ovals.

Math Problem of the Day 10

1. 14   2. 13   3. 15
4. 12   5. 13   6. 15

Quick Review
1. Students should draw 4 rectangles.
2. Students should draw 6 rectangles.
3. Students should draw 7 rectangles.

Math Problem of the Day 11

Students should draw 1 apple tree and 3 orange trees.
$1 + 3 = 4$

Quick Review
1. Students should color 3 apples.
2. Students should color 7 oranges.

Math Problem of the Day 12

Students should draw 2 apple seeds and 7 pumpkin seeds.
$2 + 7 = 9$

Quick Review

1. Students should color 8 apples.
2. Students should color 5 pumpkins.

Math Problem of the Day 13

Students should draw a set of 4 acorns and a set of 3 acorns.

$4 + 3 = 7$

Quick Review

1. Students should color 9 acorns.
2. Students should color 4 acorns.

Math Problem of the Day 14

Students should draw a set of 5 pears and a set of 3 pears.
$5 + 3 = 8$

Quick Review

1. Students should color 10 pears.
2. Students should color 2 pears.

Math Problem of the Day 15

Students should draw a set of 3 large strawberries and a set of 6 small strawberries.
$3 + 6 = 9$

Quick Review

1. Students should color 6 strawberries.
2. Students should color 11 strawberries.

Math Problem of the Day 16

$9 - 3 = 6$

Quick Review

1. 2; Students should cross out 5 pencils.
2. 2; Students should cross out 8 pencils.

Math Problem of the Day 17

$7 - 4 = 3$

Quick Review

1. 5; Students should cross out 1 pair of scissors.
2. 3; Students should cross out 6 scissors.

Math Problem of the Day 18

$13 - 6 = 7$

Quick Review

1. 3; Students should cross out 2 crayon boxes.
2. 3; Students should cross out 9 crayon boxes.

Math Problem of the Day 19

$14 - 9 = 5$

Quick Review

1. 5; Students should cross out 3 glue bottles.
2. 2; Students should cross out 2 glue bottles.

Math Problem of the Day 20

$18 - 9 = 9$

Quick Review

1. 8; Students should cross out 7 pencils.
2. 5; Students should cross out 6 pencils.

Math Problem of the Day 21

1. 3   2. 2   3. 2
4. 1   5. 6   6. 2

Quick Review

1. 1
2. 2

Math Problem of the Day 22

1. 3   2. 1   3. 2
4. 1   5. 2   6. 5

Quick Review

1. 5
2. 1

Math Problem of the Day 23

1. 6   2. 7   3. 10
4. 3   5. 5   6. 5

Quick Review

1. 5
2. 3

Math Problem of the Day 24

1. 4   2. 8   3. 6
4. 5   5. 6   6. 6

Quick Review

1. 5
2. 5

Math Problem of the Day 25

1. 7   2. 6   3. 6
4. 8   5. 7   6. 9

Quick Review

1. 4
2. 8

Math Problem of the Day 26

Students should draw 10 cookies, then cross out 6.

$10 - 6 = 4$

Quick Review

1. 19, 18
2. 12, 10
3. 9, 8
4. 4, 2

Math Problem of the Day 27

Students should draw 6 ice cream cones, then cross out 2.

$6 - 2 = 4$

Quick Review

1. 16, 14
2. 11, 10
3. 18, 16
4. 12, 11

Math Problem of the Day 28

Students should draw 8 cups of milk, then cross out 3.

$8 - 3 = 5$

Quick Review

1. 2, 1
2. 7, 6
3. 10, 8
4. 15, 14

Math Problem of the Day 29

Students should draw 9 grapes, then cross out 2.

$9 - 2 = 7$

Quick Review

1. 12, 10
2. 17, 14
3. 20, 18
4. 13, 11

Math Problem of the Day 30

Students should draw 7 cupcakes, then cross out 4.

$7 - 4 = 3$

Quick Review

1. 13, 12
2. 5, 4
3. 19, 18
4. 8, 7

Math Problem of the Day 31

1. >   2. >   3. <
4. <   5. >   6. <

Quick Review

1. Students should color the 3rd apple.
2. Students should color the 1st apple.
3. Students should color the 2nd apple.

Math Problem of the Day 32

1. <   2. >   3. <
4. >   5. >   6. <

Quick Review

1. Students should color the 4th grape.
2. Students should color the 6th grape.
3. Students should color the 5th grape.

Math Problem of the Day 33

1. <   2. <   3. >
4. >   5. <   6. >

Quick Review

1. 27
2. 39
3. 49
4. 29

Math Problem of the Day 34

1. <   2. >   3. <
4. <   5. >   6. >

Quick Review

1. 88
2. 99
3. 79
4. 78

Math Problem of the Day 35

Students should circle 2, 4, 6, 8, and 10.

2, 4, 6, 8, 10

Quick Review

1. 4
2. 8
3. 8
4. 2

Math Problem of the Day 36

Students should draw an X on 1, 3, 5, 7, and 9.

1, 3, 5, 7, 9

Quick Review

1. 3
2. 7
3. 1, 3
4. 7, 9

Math Problem of the Day 37

Students should circle 20, 34, 46, 58, and 62.

Students should draw an X on 15, 27, 59, 81, and 93.

Quick Review

1. 4
2. 3
3. 4

Math Problem of the Day 38

Students should circle 9.

Quick Review

1. 3
2. 6
3. 9
4. 8
5. 2

Math Problem of the Day 39

Students should circle 14.

Quick Review

1. 7
2. 4
3. 5
4. 1
5. 10

Math Problem of the Day 40

Students should color 38.

Quick Review

1. <
2. <
3. >
4. <

Math Problem of the Day 41

Students should color 73.

Quick Review

1. >
2. <
3. >
4. <

Math Problem of the Day 42

Students should color 33.

Quick Review

1. 10
2. 11
3. 20
4. 12
5. 50

Math Problem of the Day 43

Students should color 90.

Quick Review

1. 80
2. 60
3. 90
4. 70
5. 30

Math Problem of the Day 44

Students should circle two sets of ten spiders.

2 tens, 5 ones

25

Quick Review

Math Problem of the Day 45

Students should circle three sets of ten ladybugs.

3 tens, 8 ones

38

Quick Review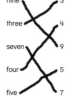

Math Problem of the Day 46

Students should circle five sets of ten bees.

5 tens, 1 ones

51

Quick Review

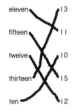

Math Problem of the Day 47

Students should circle seven sets of ten snails.

7 tens, 0 ones

70

Quick Review

Math Problem of the Day 48

Students should draw 42 raindrops in 4 sets of tens and 2 ones.

Quick Review

1. 6, 6
2. 5, 5
3. 10, 10

Math Problem of the Day 49

Students should draw 59 leaves in 5 sets of tens and 9 ones.

Quick Review

1. 9, 9
2. 9, 9
3. 7, 7

Math Problem of the Day 50

Students should draw 80 snowballs in 8 sets of tens and 0 ones.

Quick Review

1. 11, 11
2. 17, 17
3. 10, 10

Math Problem of the Day 51

H O W   M A N Y   D A Y S   I N   O N E   W E E K?

7

Quick Review

1. 67
2. 32

Math Problem of the Day 52

H O W   M A N Y   M O N T H S   I N   A   Y E A R?

12

Quick Review

1. 29
2. 94

Math Problem of the Day 53

H O W   M A N Y   H O U R S   I N   A   D A Y?

24

Quick Review

1. 13
2. 55

Math Problem of the Day 54

H O W   M A N Y   S E A S O N S   I N   A   Y E A R?

4

Quick Review

1. 1, 7
2. 3, 5

Math Problem of the Day 55

H O W   O L D   A R E   Y O U?

Students should write their age on the line.

Quick Review

1. 9, 2
2. 0, 6

Math Problem of the Day 56

4. Students should use two shapes to draw an AB pattern.

Quick Review

triangles: 5

squares: 4

circles: 3

Math Problem of the Day 57

1.

2. | | —

3. ▽ ▽△

4. Students should use two shapes to draw an AAB pattern.

Quick Review
Students should color the stars one color, the pentagons another color, and the hearts a third color.

Math Problem of the Day 58

1. ? ⌐ ⌐

2. ☼ ? ?

3. ▷ ▽ ▽

4. Students should use three shapes to draw an ABB pattern.

Quick Review
Odd numbers: 1, 3, 5, 7, 9
Even numbers: 2, 4, 6, 8

Math Problem of the Day 59

1. ▢ △ ○

2. ♡ ⌒ ◇

3. ☺ ☺ ☹

4. Students should use three shapes to draw an ABC pattern.

Quick Review
Students should draw an X on the tie with small dots.

Math Problem of the Day 60

1. ☆ ☽ ☆

2. ⌂ ⌂ ♣

3. ∧ — ∨

4. Students should draw any pattern of their choice, following the AB, AAB, ABB, or ABC pattern.

Quick Review
Students should draw an X on the crayon.

Math Problem of the Day 61
1. A, B, A, B
2. A, B, A, A, B
3. B, B, A, B, B

Quick Review
1. 74
2. 86
3. 39

Math Problem of the Day 62
1. B, C, A, B, C
2. B, B, A, B, B
3. A, B, A, B

Quick Review
1. 65
2. 91
3. 42

Math Problem of the Day 63
1. 1, 2, 1, 2
2. 2, 2, 1, 2, 2
3. 1, 2, 1, 1, 2

Quick Review
1. 91
2. 65
3. 14
4. 58

Math Problem of the Day 64
1. 2, 3, 1, 2, 3
2. 2, 2, 1, 2, 2
3. 1, 2, 2

Quick Review
1. Students should circle 87.
2. Students should circle 42.
3. Students should circle 13.

Math Problem of the Day 65
1. Students should draw four circles, five circles, and six circles on the lines.
2. 4, 5, 6, 7, 8
3. D, E, F, G, H
4. Students should draw a bigger box on each line.

Quick Review
Students should color all the star buttons one color, the diamond buttons a second color, and the heart buttons a third color.

Math Problem of the Day 66

1. AAB
2. ABB
3. ABC

Quick Review

1. Students should circle the small square.
2. Students should circle the circle.
3. Students should circle the star.

Math Problem of the Day 67

1. Students should use two of the shapes to make an AAB pattern.
2. Students should use all three shapes to make an ABC pattern.

Quick Review

1. 8
2. 7
3. 20
4. 3
5. 3

Math Problem of the Day 68

Students should use the shapes to draw a house.

Quick Review

1. square: 4
   triangle: 3
   rectangle: 4
2. Students should color the three small triangles.

Math Problem of the Day 69

Students should use the shapes to draw a train.

Quick Review

1. Students should color the square (on the right).
2. Students should color the circle (on the left).
3. Students should color the rectangle (on the left).

Math Problem of the Day 70

Students should use the shapes to draw a space creature.

Quick Review

1. Students should color the three large squares.
2. 4

Math Problem of the Day 71

Students should draw only circles, squares, and triangles on the picture frame. They should draw a self-portrait in the frame.

Quick Review

1. Students should draw a large and small square.
2. Students should draw two circles of the same size.

Math Problem of the Day 72

Students should color the picture according to the color key.

Quick Review

1. Students should draw a square.
2. Students should draw a heart.
3. Students should draw a diamond.

Math Problem of the Day 73

Students should color the picture according to the color key.

Quick Review

1. Students should draw a triangle.
2. Students should draw a square, rectangle, trapezoid, parallelogram, or rhomboid.
3. Students should draw a different four-sided shape from the one drawn in 2.

Math Problem of the Day 74

Students should draw an item in each box that corresponds to the shape named at the top of the box.

Quick Review

1. Students should color the last shape.
2. Students should color the middle shape.
3. Students should color the first shape.

Math Problem of the Day 75

1. Students should draw a diagonal line from one corner of the square to the opposite corner.
2. Students should draw a diagonal line from each top corner to its opposite corner.

Quick Review

1. 4
2. 4
3. 6

Math Problem of the Day 76

1. Students should draw a line from one corner of the triangle to the opposite side.
2. Students should draw three lines from one corner of the triangle to the opposite side. Or they might draw an upside-down triangle inside the large triangle, making sure each corner touches a side of the larger triangle.

Quick Review

1. 3
2. 4
3. 5

Math Problem of the Day 77

1. Students should draw a vertical line down the middle of the rectangle.
2. Students should draw a diagonal line from one corner of the rectangle to the opposite corner.

Quick Review

1. 0
2. 4
3. 3

Math Problem of the Day 78

1. Students should draw a vertical line from the top to bottom corner of the diamond. Or they might draw a horizontal line from the left to right corner of the diamond.
2. Students should draw a diagonal line through the middle of the diamond from one side to the opposite side.

Quick Review

1. Students should circle *cone*.
2. Students should circle *cylinder*.
3. Students should circle *cube*.

Math Problem of the Day 79

Students should draw the shape in the size indicated in each box.

Quick Review

Math Problem of the Day 80

Students should draw the other half of each shape.

Quick Review

triangles: 5
squares: 2
rectangles: 3

Math Problem of the Day 81

Students should make a square on the right that is identical in size to the square on the left.
1. Students should circle *square*.
2. 16

Quick Review

1. no
2. yes
3. yes

Math Problem of the Day 82

Students should make a small square on the left and a larger square on the right.

1. Students' answers will vary according to the size of their squares.
2. Students should draw a line either vertically or horizontally to divide each square in half.

Quick Review

1. no
2. yes
3. yes

Math Problem of the Day 83

Students should make a rectangle on the right that is identical to the rectangle on the left.
1. Students should circle *rectangle*.
2. 16

Quick Review

1. Students should draw a line to divide the football in half vertically or horizontally.
2. Students should draw a line to divide the baseball in half vertically or horizontally.
3. Students should draw a line to divide the baseball diamond in half vertically.

Math Problem of the Day 84

Students should make a large rectangle on the left and a smaller rectangle on the right.

1. Students' answers will vary according to the size of their rectangles.
2. Students should draw a line either vertically or horizontally to divide each rectangle in half.

Quick Review

1. Students should draw a line to divide the crayon in half horizontally.
2. Students should draw a line to divide the ruler in half vertically or horizontally.
3. Students should draw a line to divide the glue bottle in half vertically.

Math Problem of the Day 85

Students should make a triangle on the right that is identical to the triangle on the left.
1. Students should circle *triangle*.
2. 8

Quick Review

1. Students should draw a line to divide the glass in half vertically.
2. Students should draw a line to divide the jar in half vertically.
3. Students should draw a line to divide the bowl in half vertically.

Math Problem of the Day 86

Students should make a rectangle on the left and a triangle on the right.

1. Students answers will vary according to the size of their rectangle and triangle.

2. Students should draw a line either vertically or horizontally to divide the rectangle in half. They should draw a vertical line to divide the triangle in half.

Quick Review

hearts: 3

stars: 2

diamonds: 3

Math Problem of the Day 87

Quick Review

1. Students should circle *flip*.
2. Students should circle *turn*.
3. Students should circle *slide*.

Math Problem of the Day 88

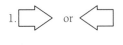

Quick Review

1. Students should circle *turn*.
2. Students should circle *slide*.
3. Students should circle *flip*.

Math Problem of the Day 89

Quick Review

1. Students should circle *flip*.
2. Students should circle *slide*.
3. Students should circle *flip*.

Math Problem of the Day 90

2. Students' shapes will vary according to how they put together the triangles and squares.

Quick Review

1. Students should draw an identical heart.

2. Students should draw a rectangle standing on one short end.

3. Students should draw the triangle upside down or with the right angle on the right side.

Math Problem of the Day 91

1. Students should circle *desk*.
2. Students should circle *door*.
3. Students should circle *chalkboard*.
4. Students should circle *clock*.

Quick Review

1. Students should draw a line that extends up from the dot.

2. Students should draw a line that extends right from the dot.

Math Problem of the Day 92

1. Students should circle *playground*.
2. Students should circle *apartments*.
3. Students should circle *diner*.
4. Students should circle *motel*.

Quick Review

1. Students should draw a line that extends left from the dot.

2. Students should draw a line that extends down from the dot.

Math Problem of the Day 93

1. Students should circle *east*.
2. Students should circle *south*.
3. Students should circle *west*.
4. Students should circle *monkeys*.

Quick Review

1. Students should circle *east*.
2. Students should circle *south*.
3. Students should circle *west*.

Math Problem of the Day 94

1. Students should circle *west*.
2. Students should circle *south*.
3. Students should circle *east*.
4. Students should circle *south*.

Quick Review

1. Students should draw an arrow that points up.
2. Students should draw an arrow that points right.
3. Students should draw an arrow that points down.

Math Problem of the Day 95

1. Flora
2. Abe
3. Bea
4. Dean
5. Cassie

Quick Review

1. Students should circle *north*.
2. Students should draw an arrow that points left.

Math Problem of the Day 96

4D: duck
2C: fish
1B: turtle
3A: snake

Quick Review

1. 2, 5, 9
2. 1, 4 ,7
3. 8, 11, 15

Math Problem of the Day 97

2A: ball
4B: kite
3C: boat
1D: cloud

Quick Review

1. 9, 15, 20
2. 1, 10, 18
3. 2, 4, 6

Math Problem of the Day 98

3C: book
1A: door
4D: desk
2B: flag

Quick Review

1. 30, 40, 50
2. 7, 17, 27
3. 33, 66, 99

Math Problem of the Day 99

bus: 2A
bike: 4B
train: 2D
plane: 1C

Quick Review

1. 21, 23, 24   3. 17, 19
2. 37, 40, 41   4. 50, 52, 53

Math Problem of the Day 100

circle: 1B
star: 4A
heart: 2C
square: 3D

Quick Review

1. 8, 7, 6   3. 2, 1, 0
2. 30, 31, 32   4. 53, 54, 55

Math Problem of the Day 101

1. 10; Students should draw 6 candies plus 4 candies.
2. 8; Students should draw 5 cookies plus 3 cookies.

Quick Review

1. 2
2. 2, 4
3. 2, 4, 6

Math Problem of the Day 102

1. 6; Students should draw 4 balls plus 2 balls.
2. 7; Students should draw 3 dolls plus 4 dolls.

Quick Review

1. 5, 10
2. 5, 10, 15, 20
3. 5, 10, 15

Math Problem of the Day 103

1. 8; Students should draw 3 flowers plus 5 flowers.
2. 10; Students should draw 7 leaves plus 3 leaves

Quick Review

1. 12
2. 8
3. 24

Math Problem of the Day 104

1. 16; Students should draw 10 ants plus 6 ants.
2. 15; Students should draw 7 snakes plus 8 snakes.

Quick Review

1. 5
2. 6
3. 10

Math Problem of the Day 105

1. 6; Students should draw 10 crayons, then cross out 4.
2. 2; Students should draw 8 rulers, then cross out 6.

Quick Review

1. 3, 2
2. 9, 8, 7
3. 13, 12, 11
4. 6, 5, 4

Math Problem of the Day 106

1. 3; Students should draw 12 slices of pie, then cross out 9.
2. 6; Students should draw 17 bags of popcorn, then cross out 11.

Quick Review

1. 7; Students should draw an X on 3 cupcakes.
2. 3; Students should draw an X on 5 ice cream cones.
3. 4; Students should draw an X on 9 lollipops.

Math Problem of the Day 107

1. 12; Students should draw 18 bones, then cross out 6.
2. 6; Students should draw 13 acorns, then cross out 7.

Quick Review

1. $8 - 3 = 5, 8 - 5 = 3$
2. $8 - 2 = 6, 8 - 6 = 2$

Math Problem of the Day 108

1. 2; Students should draw 9 cups, then cross out 7.
2. 6; Students should draw 11 cans, then cross out 5.

Quick Review

1. $9 - 5 = 4, 9 - 4 = 5$
2. $10 - 3 = 7, 10 - 7 = 3$

Math Problem of the Day 109

1. Students should circle the dog.
2. Students should circle Tim.

Quick Review

1. Students should color the hexagon.
2. Students should color the triangle at the top right.

Math Problem of the Day 110

1. Students should circle Pam.
2. Students should circle the paper.

Quick Review

1. Students should color the rabbit.
2. Students should color the baby.

Math Problem of the Day 111

1. Students should circle the tub.
2. Students should circle the quarter.

Quick Review

1. Students should color the last rope.
2. Students should color the caterpillar.

Math Problem of the Day 112

Students should draw seven people with cookies.
7

Quick Review

1. 10
2. 10
3. 6
4. 9
5. 7
6. 11

Math Problem of the Day 113

Students should draw a hand with two rings on each finger.
10

Quick Review

1. 9
2. 7
3. 12
4. 8
5. 13
6. 18

Math Problem of the Day 114

Students should draw 16 balloons, then cross out 8 balloons and then 4 more.
4

Quick Review

1. 3
2. 15
3. 5
4. 16
5. 13
6. 11

Math Problem of the Day 115

Students should draw 20 cards, then cross out 10 cards and then 6 more.
4

Quick Review

1. $5 + 8 = 13$
2. $5 + 7 = 12$
3. $9 + 6 = 15$

Math Problem of the Day 116

1. 7
2. 6
3. 5
4. 4

Quick Review

1. Students should circle the bottom nail.
2. Students should circle the bottom screwdriver.

Math Problem of the Day 117

1. 10
2. 7
3. 3
4. 11

Quick Review

1. Students should circle the middle snake.
2. Students should circle the top ribbon.

Math Problem of the Day 118

1. 4
2. 5
3. 3
4. 2

Quick Review

1. Students should circle the paintbrush.
2. Students should circle the glue stick.

Math Problem of the Day 119

1. 3
2. 4
3. 6
4. 7

Quick Review

1. 4
2. 3

Math Problem of the Day 120

1. 8
2. 4
3. 3

Quick Review

1. Students should circle the mop on the left.
2. Students should circle the paintbrush on the left.

Math Problem of the Day 121

1. 7 days
2. Sunday
3. Saturday
4. 30 days

Quick Review

1. 2:00
2. 4:00
3. 11:00
4. 7:00

Math Problem of the Day 122

1. Tuesday
2. Thursday
3. 31 days
4. 4 Saturdays

Quick Review

1. 3:30
2. 8:30
3. 10:30
4. 1:30

Math Problem of the Day 123

Students should fill in the missing numbers between 1 and 31 on the calendar.

1. Wednesday
2. 31 days
3. Monday
4. 5 Wednesdays

Quick Review

1. Students should draw the hour hand pointing to the 3.
2. Students should draw the hour hand pointing to the 5.
3. Students should draw the hour hand pointing to the 9.
4. Students should draw the hour hand pointing to the 10.

Math Problem of the Day 124

Students should write the name of the current month on the line above the calendar and then fill in the dates on the calendar to correspond to the days of that month.

1–4. Students should use the information on their calendar to answer each question.

Quick Review

1. Students should draw the hour hand pointing between the 3 and 4.
2. Students should draw the hour hand pointing between the 7 and 8.
3. Students should draw the hour hand pointing between the 4 and 5.
4. Students should draw the hour hand pointing between the 6 and 7.

Math Problem of the Day 125

1. February 18
2. soccer practice
3. February 14
4. Groundhog Day

Quick Review

1. Students should draw the minute hand pointing to the 12 and the hour hand pointing to the 4.
2. Students should draw the minute hand pointing to the 6 and the hour hand pointing between the 9 and 10.
3. Students should draw the minute hand pointing to the 6 and the hour hand pointing between the 11 and 12.
4. Students should draw the minute hand pointing to the 12 and the hour hand pointing to the 1.

Math Problem of the Day 126

Students should draw any combination of coins that equals 10¢, then draw 5 pennies.

15¢

Quick Review

1. <
2. =
3. <

Math Problem of the Day 127

Students should circle the nickel and 5 pennies (lower right corner).

Quick Review

1. <
2. >
3. >

Math Problem of the Day 128

Students should draw five pennies, one dime, and two nickels.

25¢

Quick Review

1. >
2. =
3. <

Math Problem of the Day 129

Students should circle the kite.

Quick Review

1. >
2. <
3. =

Math Problem of the Day 130

1. 25¢   3. 40¢
2. 40¢   4. 40¢

Quick Review

1. =
2. <
3. <

Math Problem of the Day 131

1. 7, 3, 4
2. snakes
3. 14

Quick Review

1. 8   3. 9
2. 10   4. 7

Math Problem of the Day 132

1. 8, 6, 9
2. 15
3. 17
4. 3

Quick Review

1. 10
2. 6
3. 8
4. 9

Math Problem of the Day 133

1. 3, 6, 4
2. 3
3. 1
4. 10

Quick Review

1. 5
2. 10
3. 13
4. 7

Math Problem of the Day 134

Students should color 6 boxes for the car and 4 boxes for the truck.

1. 4 trucks, 6 cars, 4 + 6 = 10
2. 6 − 4 = 2

Quick Review

1. 6
2. 9
3. 12
4. 15

Math Problem of the Day 135

Students should color 4 boxes for the shirt, 3 boxes for the shorts, and 5 boxes for the hat.

1. 5 hats, 3 shorts, 4 shirts
2. 12
3. $5 - 3 = 2$

Quick Review

1. 14
2. 11
3. 9

Math Problem of the Day 136

Students should color 5 boxes for the football, 8 boxes for the basketball, and 2 boxes for the baseball.

1. 15
2. $5 - 2 = 3$
3. $8 - 5 = 3$

Quick Review

1. 7
2. 11
3. 10

Math Problem of the Day 137

Students should color 3 boxes for the pig, 8 boxes for the cow, and 5 boxes for the hen.

1. Students should circle the hen.
2. 5
3. 3

Quick Review

1. 14
2. 13
3. 11

Math Problem of the Day 138

Students should color 3 boxes for the dog, 5 boxes for the cat, and 4 boxes for the turtle.

1. $4 - 3 = 1$
2. $5 + 3 = 8$

Quick Review

1. 12   3. 20
2. 16   4. 17

Math Problem of the Day 139

Students should color 6 boxes for the lollipop, 3 boxes for the ice cream cone, and 4 boxes for the cupcake.

1. $6 - 4 = 2$
2. $6 + 3 = 9$

Quick Review

1. 18   2. 14   3. 19

Math Problem of the Day 140

Students should color 8 boxes for the dog and 7 boxes for the cat.

1. 8, 7
2. $8 + 7 = 15$
3. $8 - 7 = 1$

Quick Review

1. 7   3. 11
2. 3   4. 21

Math Problem of the Day 141

Students should color 5 boxes for the cap, 9 boxes for the crown, and 6 boxes for the helmet.

1. $9 - 5 = 4$
2. $6 - 5 = 1$
3. 20

Quick Review

1. 25
2. 23
3. 27

Math Problem of the Day 142

Students should color 2 boxes for the standing bear, 5 boxes for the sitting bear, and 8 boxes for the sleeping bear.

1. Students should circle the sleeping bear.
2. 15
3. $8 - 5 = 3$

Quick Review

1. 9, 9
2. 8, 8
3. 7, 7

Math Problem of the Day 143

Students should color a box that corresponds to each classmate's response.

1–4. Students should use the information on their graph to answer each question.

Quick Review

1. 10, 10
2. 10, 10
3. 10, 10

Math Problem of the Day 144

Students should color a box that corresponds to each classmate's response.

1–4. Students should use the information on their graph to answer each question.

Quick Review

1. $3 + 2 = 5$
2. $6 + 4 = 10$

Math Problem of the Day 145

Students should color a box that corresponds to each classmate's response.

1–3. Students should use the information on their graph to answer each question.

Quick Review

1. 卌 卌 ||| 3. 卌 卌 卌 卌

2. 卌 卌 卌 | 4. 卌 卌 卌 ||||

Math Problem of the Day 146

Students should draw tally marks and color a box that corresponds to each classmate's response.

1–3. Students should use the information on their graph to answer each question.

Quick Review

1. 卌 卌 | 3. ||||

2. 卌 || 4. 卌 |||

Math Problem of the Day 147

Students should draw tally marks and color a box that corresponds to each classmate's response.

1–3. Students should use the information on their graph to answer each question.

Quick Review

1. 卌 卌   3. 卌 ||||

2. 卌 卌 卌   4. 卌 卌 ||

Math Problem of the Day 148

Students should draw tally marks and color a box that corresponds to each classmate's response.

1–3. Students should use the information on their graph to answer each question.

Quick Review

1. 13, 13   3. 13, 13

2. 11, 11   4. 12, 12

Math Problem of the Day 149

Students should color a box that corresponds to each classmate's response.

1–4. Students should use the information on their graph to answer each question.

Quick Review

3 bats

6 wings

6 eyes

6 legs

6 ears

3 heads

Math Problem of the Day 150

Students should color a box that corresponds to each classmate's response.

1–3. Students should use the information on their graph to answer each question.

Quick Review

8 eyes

4 spiders

32 legs

4 bodies

4 heads

Math Problem of the Day 151

Students should color a box that corresponds to each classmate's response.

1–3. Students should use the information on their graph to answer each question.

Quick Review

6 ears

3 noses

12 legs

6 eyes

12 feet

Math Problem of the Day 152

Students should color a box that corresponds to each classmate's response.

1–2. Students should use the information on their graph to answer each question.

Quick Review

4 eyes

8 legs

8 spots

2 noses

4 ears

2 tails

Math Problem of the Day 153

Students should color a box that corresponds to each side the penny lands on.

1–3. Students should use the information on their graph to answer each question.

Quick Review

12 legs

4 wings

12 spots

4 antennae

2 heads

Math Problem of the Day 154

1. green: B; yellow: C
2. Students should circle *A*.

Quick Review

1. 7	2. 6	3. 5
4. 4	5. 3	6. 2

Math Problem of the Day 155

Students should color the large section of the spinner blue and the small section red.

1. Students should color a box that corresponds to each color the spinner lands on.
2. Students should use the information on their graph to answer the question.

Quick Review

1. 2	2. 3	3. 4
4. 5	5. 6	6. 7

Math Problem of the Day 156

Students should color half the spinner red and the other half yellow.

1. Students should color a box that corresponds to each color the spinner lands on.
2. Students should use the information on their graph to answer the question.

Quick Review

1. 8	2. 7	3. 6
4. 9	5. 10	6. 5

Math Problem of the Day 157

1. 4	2. 3	3. 1
4. 3	5. 6	

Quick Review

1. Students should circle 2, 4.
2. Students should circle 4, 3.
3. Students should circle 4, 4.
4. Students should circle 5, 4.

Math Problem of the Day 158

1. 2	2. 5	3. 6
4. 3	5. 9	

Quick Review

1. Students should circle 3, 1.
2. Students should circle 3, 3.
3. Students should circle 6, 3.
4. Students should circle 5, 3.

Math Problem of the Day 159

1. 3
2. 2
3. 1
4. pencil
5. 8

Quick Review

1. 5, 5
2. 8, 3
3. 5, 7
4. 9, 4

Math Problem of the Day 160

1. 3
2. 3
3. 4
4. doll
5. 12

Quick Review

1. 9, 3
2. 7, 6
3. 7, 7
4. 9, 6

Math Problem of the Day 161

1. 3
2. 1
3. 2
4. 4
5. bus

Quick Review

1. 7, 9
2. 8, 9
3. 12, 6
4. 11, 8

Math Problem of the Day 162

1. one
2. two
3. ½
4. one

Quick Review

1. Students should circle $1/4$.
2. Students should circle $3/4$.
3. Students should circle $1/3$.

Math Problem of the Day 163

1. two
2. $^1/_3$
3. three
4. $^1/_4$

Quick Review

1. Students should circle $^4/_6$.
2. Students should circle $^1/_3$.
3. Students should circle $^1/_2$.

Math Problem of the Day 164

Students should mark an X on all the critters except the spider.

1. spider
2. Students should write a new clue about the spider.

Quick Review

1. 3
2. 8
3. turtles

Math Problem of the Day 165

Students should mark an X on all the vehicles except the wagon.

1. wagon
2. Students should write a new clue about the wagon.

Quick Review

1. Wed.
2. 12

Math Problem of the Day 166

1. Lisa
2. Students should write a new clue about Lisa.

Quick Review

1. green
2. 4
3. 14

Math Problem of the Day 167

1. strawberry
2. Students should write a new clue about the strawberry.

Quick Review

1. Abe: 25; Ben: 15
2. Abe

Math Problem of the Day 168

1. kangaroo
2. Students should write a new clue about the kangaroo.

Quick Review

1. 50
2. 40
3. 50 – 40 = 10

Math Problem of the Day 169

1. The apples in the circle have been cut and have seeds.
2. The apples outside the circle are whole apples.
3. 16

Quick Review

1. fruit
2. apples: 2; bananas: 4; pears: 2
3. 8

Math Problem of the Day 170

1. The ties in the circle have dots.
2. The ties outside the circle have stripes.
3. 10

Quick Review

1. homes
2. by 4s
3. house: 4; condo: 8; cabin: 4

Math Problem of the Day 171

1. The hearts in the circle have black borders.
2. The hearts around the circle have lace borders.
3. 10

Quick Review

1. trees
2. by 2s
3. pine: 4; maple: 6; oak: 8

Math Problem of the Day 172

1. The flags in the circle have an even number of stars.
2. The flags outside the circle have an odd number of stars.
3. All the flags have stars on them.

Quick Review

1. flowers
2. by 3s
3. rose: 3; tulip: 6; daisy: 3

Math Problem of the Day 173

1. The animals in the circle are water animals.
2. The animals outside the circle are land animals.
3. All the animals have a mouth and eyes.

Quick Review

1. vehicles
2. by 10s
3. cars: 40; trucks: 30; vans: 50

Math Problem of the Day 174

5th floor: Matt
4th floor: Gina
3rd floor: Lisa
2nd floor: Ann
1st floor: Bob
Bob lives on the 1st floor.

Quick Review

1. $1 + 2 = 3$; $2 + 1 = 3$; $3 - 1 = 2$; $3 - 2 = 1$
2. $2 + 3 = 5$; $3 + 2 = 5$; $5 - 2 = 3$; $5 - 3 = 2$

Math Problem of the Day 175

1st: Amy
2nd: Ned
3rd: Tim
4th: Jen
5th: Dan
Jen was 4th in line.

Quick Review

1. $3 + 4 = 7$; $4 + 3 = 7$; $7 - 3 = 4$; $7 - 4 = 3$
2. $3 + 5 = 8$; $5 + 3 = 8$; $8 - 3 = 5$; $8 - 5 = 3$

Math Problem of the Day 176

12: Bert
14: Lee
16: Norma
18: Candy
20: Ron
Candy lives in house 18.

Quick Review

1. $4 + 5 = 9$; $5 + 4 = 9$; $9 - 4 = 5$; $9 - 5 = 4$
2. $3 + 6 = 9$; $6 + 3 = 9$; $9 - 3 = 6$; $9 - 6 = 3$

Math Problem of the Day 177

pentagon: Deb
hexagon: Barb
triangle: Chad
star: Steve
circle: Fred
Chad has the triangle.

Quick Review

1. $2 + 5 = 7$; $5 + 2 = 7$; $7 - 2 = 5$; $7 - 5 = 2$
2. $3 + 7 = 10$; $7 + 3 = 10$; $10 - 3 = 7$; $10 - 7 = 3$

Math Problem of the Day 178

helmet: Phil
tall hat: Nicole
crown: Sasha

Quick Review

1. Students should circle the hippo.
2. Students should circle the bus.
3. Students should circle the baseball.
4. Students should circle the doghouse.

Math Problem of the Day 179

milk: Betty
water: Jim
fruit juice: Pat

Quick Review

1. Students should circle the cat.
2. Students should circle the bed.
3. Students should circle the pumpkin.
4. Students should circle the apple.

Math Problem of the Day 180

curly hair: Brenda
long hair: Grace
short hair: Stacy

Quick Review

1. Students should circle the sandals.
2. Students should circle the pint.
3. Students should circle the bookbag.
4. Students should circle the feather.